ACKNOWLEDGE

CU00590406

Over the years a number of individual people ha͞
me with items of information relating to partic
am grateful to them all and sincerely hope I h͞
following list:

Mr J Birkby	Mr J H Poyser
The Revd J Bland	Mr M Renshaw
Dr C Charlton	The late Mr E R Robbins
Mr J H C Davies	Mr E R Stow
The Revd J O Drackley	The Revd Dr N Thistlethwaite
The late Mr H Hitchcock	Mrs B Thorpe
Mr P Johnson	Mr D C Wickens
The late Mr D S Makin	Mr R Wood

Rodney Tomkins, *Duffield, May 1995*

37, QUEEN STREET, DERBY   Telephone 730y3.

(Opposite St. Michael's Church),

.... *190*

Dr. to J. H. ADKINS,

❋ Organ Builder and Tuner.

....

Specifications & Estimates for New & Second-hand Organs, Re-constructions, Enlargements, &c., Gratis.

TUNINGS BY YEARLY CONTRACT.   **HIGHEST LOCAL REFERENCES.**

Published by Scarthin Books, Cromford, Derbyshire, 1995

ISBN 0 907758 88 6

*COVER PHOTOGRAPHS. FRONT: The 1853 Holt Organ at St. Peter's, Belper
      – by W. Attenborough*
      *BACK: Milford, Shaw Lane Methodist Chapel
           (author's photograph)*

A much-travelled instrument – the 1874 Grunwell in Milford Church

PIPE ORGANS
IN CHURCHES AND CHAPELS
of the
DERBYSHIRE DERWENT
and
ECCLESBOURNE VALLEYS
from Darley Abbey to Darley Dale

by

RODNEY TOMKINS

Scarthin Books
1995

PREFACE

At the start of the twentieth century Derbyshire may have possessed well over 1,500 places of worship – the large majority of these having pipe organs. But as we now approach the end of that same century, the number of churches and chapels (especially the latter) has been drastically reduced, the present total being considerably less than 1,000 – and still falling. Of those buildings that remain, a small but significant number have replaced their pipe organs with electronic ones – the motives for such exchanges being occasionally musical, sometimes spatial, more often than not financial. A rough estimate would leave us, by the end of the millennium, with approximately 250 Anglican pipe organs and a similar number in the combined churches of other denominations.

Having collected over the years a vast amount of material in the way of publications, documents and my own copious notes, I have felt the need to set it all out in a co-ordinated and accessible manner before it gets forgotten or lost. My initial idea was to present a comprehensive survey covering every pipe organ (hopefully both past and present) within the County as a whole. Without something like a generous travelling scholarship, however, I could not realistically envisage such a task being completed within the foreseeable future. I decided, therefore, to concentrate my research on a smaller, clearly-defined (and home-based) area stretching from the northern outskirts of Derby to the borders of the great estates in the north – an area containing three medium-sized towns and about thirty village communities, all owing their existence and their historical development to the River Derwent and its important parallel tributary, the Ecclesbourne.

Within this geographical entity I have had the pleasure of visiting nearly every place of worship with a pipe organ history. Many gems have been discovered and many good associations formed with clergy, organists and other church folk who have all been kind, helpful and welcoming. If this little book achieves anything, I hope it will be that it has contributed in some way towards an increased awareness and appreciation of our numerous churches and chapels (especially some of the smaller, less well-known ones) – not just as buildings alone but as places that can come alive with the music of so many excellent little (and not so little) instruments.

I would also thank the Clergy, Organists and others who have made me more than welcome at the various churches and chapels.

Finally, I am indebted to those who have been kind enough to spend valuable time reading the script and making helpful suggestions:

Mr George Barrass   Mr John Poyser
The Revd John Drackley   Mr Edmund Stow

and my wife, Margaret, who has not only read the script but has also accompanied me on many of the visits and has been a constant source of encouragement to me.

CONTENTS

LOCATION MAP

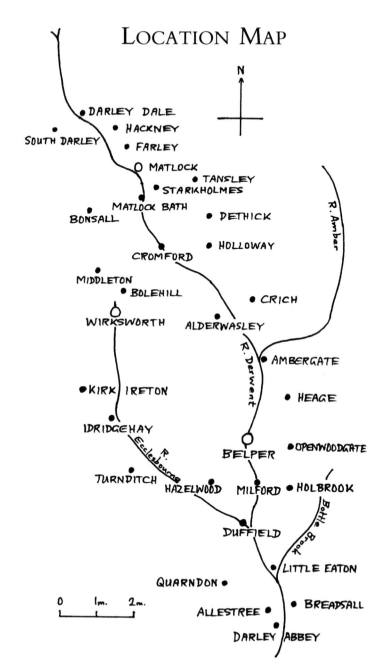

Location map of Derwent and Ecclesbourne Valleys

EXPLANATORY NOTES

SPECIFICATIONS

Though "specifications" (ie stop-lists) may not tell us everything about an organ, they are nevertheless of vital importance in assessing the style (and sometimes even the date and builder) of an instrument as well as in giving a good idea of its scope and potential. Sometimes, though, as at Over Hackney, an unprepossessing stop-list may conceal a versatile and worthwhile little organ of considerable musicality. In the descriptions of the organs the last specification quoted may not necessarily be the final one (– later alterations, if of a simple nature, being indicated in the text), since it is the earlier formats that are of historical interest and can so easily (and surprisingly quickly) become forgotten.

For those to whom the specifications are of significant interest, I would point out that, in order to achieve simplicity of presentation, I have adopted a policy of not including lists of accessories (such as registration aids) and have given the various couplers only in summarized form (– except where some non-standard feature may have demanded otherwise).

To the uninitiated I would say that, in the specifications, the figure after a stop-name indicates the length (in feet) of the bottom pipe of that particular rank. Stops marked 8 will sound at normal (ie unison) pitch; those with smaller numbers will sound at octave pitch (4) or even higher (2-2/3, 2, etc), giving various degrees of brightness to the ensemble, with the Mixture stops (compound ranks of very small pipes) providing a crown to the whole. Similarly, stops of 16ft or more will increase the profundity of the tone, especially in the pedal bass department. A casual scrutiny of the various specifications will therefore reveal that many later nineteenth and earlier twentieth century organs have a wide assortment of colourfully Romantic (and often imitative) 8ft stops of different levels of power, but that all too frequently this is at the expense of a broad Classical ensemble of pipes sounding together over a whole range of pitches.

It should be noted that many older instruments do not actually bear pitch figures on their stop-labels: in the text these numbers are therefore indicated in brackets.

COMPASS

Standard Compass (from approximately 1860's)–
Manuals from Bass-C (2 octaves below Middle-C)	56 or 58 notes
Pedal from Bass-C	30 notes

Earlier Victorian (approximately 1840's to 1870's)–
Great and Choir from Bass-C	54 notes
Swell from Tenor-C (1 octave below Middle-C)	42 notes
Pedal from Bass-C	anything from 20 to 29 notes

Pre-Victorian (until as late as 1850's)–
Great and Choir from GG (5 notes below Bass-C)	57 or 58 notes
Swell from Middle-C or Fiddle-G (5 notes below Middle-C)	29 to 34 notes
Pedal (if any) from GG	12 to 18 notes

EXTENSION ORGANS

These are instruments in which individual ranks of pipes are used for several stops, at more than one pitch and on more than one keyboard. Two of the organs described are built entirely on this principle (Allestree St Edmund and Ambergate Methodist). In many other instruments the system is used to provide additional Pedal stops (– a useful economy in both space and money).

ACTION

The means by which air is released into the pipes. It may be mechanical (also referred to as "tracker" action), pneumatic, electro-pneumatic or electric (direct).

DENOMINATIONAL ABBREVIATIONS

The following abbreviations for certain denominational church names are used in the text:

RC   Roman Catholic
UMFC   United Methodist Free Church
URC   United Reformed Church

Console of late C19th Bevington organ in Little Eaton Methodist Church (until 1981)

THE ORGANS

1 DARLEY ABBEY

The first village north of mediaeval Derby, it grew up around the Augustinian Abbey which was situated close to the Derwent in a location where the river starts to assume its scenic, contoured formation. Heavily dependent upon the Abbey, the village nevertheless remained within the Derby parish of St Alkmund and had no parochial life of its own until the early nineteenth century—by which time it had been transformed into a small, self-contained industrial cotton mill community.

ABBEY CHURCH OF ST MARY

Founded in 1137, the Abbey became prosperous and influential. After four hundred years of service it was eventually dissolved in 1540, two years after having been surrendered to the Crown Commissioners – at which point many of its furnishings, including an organ, had been sold off to Robert Sacheverall, the Vicar of Ashbourne.

One can only speculate as to the nature of such an organ. The possibilities would have been:

1   a "portative" – i.e. a small portable instrument of about two octaves which could be carried in procession – held in the arm (as in mediaeval paintings of Angel Musicians) and pumped with one hand while the other played melodically on the small keyboard;

2   a "positive" – i.e. a small free-standing organ of a type also depicted in fifteenth century paintings by such masters as van der Goes and van Eyck. Here both hands would be able to play conventionally on a keyboard of some three or four octaves while wind was pumped either by the foot or by an assistant;

3   a more substantial instrument, though probably still of only one keyboard – akin to the sole surviving British pre-Reformation organ (albeit casework only) at Old Radnor in Wales.

PARISH CHURCH OF ST MATTHEW

This prettily "Gothick" church was completed and consecrated in 1819. Its benefactor was Walter Evans, son of Thomas, creator of the mill and its associated community.

Archdeacon Butler, referring to this organ in his 1824 Visitation, says: "there is one" (and also that there is "no salary" for the organist!). The following year Alexander Buckingham, a travelling organ builder (who had in 1824 "set up" a 4-stop barrel organ for Walter Evans and who now, in 1825, was building an organ for Derby St Alkmund), appears to have inspected the church organ and claimed it to be "one of George England's make". If this is indeed correct then the instrument must have been second-hand, since the latter builder flourished in the 1760's and 70's. Buckingham may, however, have been referring to the son, George Pike England, whose work was from the late 1780's to *c*1815.

1885 Forster & Andrews Organ at St Matthew's, Darley Abbey

The England organ had the following stops (as given by Buckingham) :

GREAT (GG)		SWELL (Middle-C)	
Open Diapason (G)	(8)	Dulciana	(8)
Stop Diapason		Flute	(4)
bass & treble	(8)	Cornet (3 ranks)	
Principal	(4)	Trumpet	(8)
Flute bass & treble	(4)		
Fifteenth	(2)		
Sexqualtra bass (3 ranks)			
Cornet treble (3 ranks)			

This will no doubt be the instrument referred to in White's 1857 Directory as "a small organ". Though regarded as adequate during the earlier nineteenth century, such a specification did not meet the aspirations of the later part of the century. On completion of the church restoration of 1885-6 (paid for by Walter Evans, great-grandson of the original Thomas) a brand new organ was installed by Forster & Andrews of Hull which had the following stops :

GREAT		SWELL	
Open Diapason	8	Violin Diapason	8
Stopped Diapason	8	Salicional	8
Dulciana	8	Voix Celestes	8
Principal	4	Gemshorn	4
Waldflöte	4	Piccolo	2
Fifteenth	2	Cornopean	8
		Oboe	8
PEDAL		Tremulant	
Bourdon	16		

COUPLERS: 3 unison & Swell suboctave
COMPASS: Manuals 56: Pedal 30
ACTION: Manuals mechanical; Pedal pneumatic

This specification remained unchanged for exactly a century until an overhaul by John Corkhill of Wigan in 1986 when the Cornopean was revoiced as a Trumpet and the Oboe was replaced by a Mixture (2 ranks).

The organ is situated in a chamber on the north side of the chancel. The cantilevered front display pipes have stencilled decorations and are "free-standing" (i.e. supported from behind). The church maintains a high musical standard and the organ continues to give good service to this end.

2 ALLESTREE

Formerly a chapelry within the mediaeval parish of Markeaton (otherwise known as Mackworth), Allestree has expanded during the twentieth century to become a large residential community of over 13,000 population. In 1968 (exactly one hundred years after achieving parish status in its own right) it was incorporated into the then County Borough (now City) of Derby.

PARISH CHURCH OF ST EDMUND

Around the church can be seen a few of the older village houses. The church itself was totally rebuilt in the mid-1860's, the tower and south door alone betraying its mediaeval origin.

1977 Wood organ in St Edmund's, Allestree

The architect's plan of 1865 shows an organ in the south-east chapel – for which instrument there is an unsubstantiated date of 1859 (suggesting that it came from the old building). This was a 1-manual with one octave (thirteen notes) of pedals. We can only guess at the stops – possibly something like three 8's, two 4's and a Fifteenth 2.

No doubt charming, but inadequate for the more sophisticated notions of the later nineteenth century, it was rebuilt and enlarged in 1885 by W. Hill & Son of London. The Pedal was increased to thirty notes, a Tenor-C Clarinet was added to the Great and a new Swell was provided with the following stops:

Open Diapason	8
Salicional	8
Hohl Flute	8
Gemshorn	4
Oboe	8

Although of top-class provenance, the instrument proved troublesome and there followed a succession of operations by various builders, the first of which was barely seven years after the Hill rebuild:

1892   "New rebuilt organ" by Noble of Derby: no details are known except that it was dedicated on 16th April.

1906   Renovated by J H Adkins of Derby: "new bellows, action fittings, etc".

1925   Overhauled by Adkins.

1936   Reconstructed and enlarged by Adkins and placed on a raised platform – probably to avoid the dry rot that had manifest itself. The following specification is taken from the Scotchbrook Notebooks (– but see note at back, under "The Sources", for a comment about the accuracy of this one in particular).

GREAT		SWELL	
Open Diapason	8	Violin Diapason	8
Open Diapason	8	Gedact	8
Dulciana	8	Gamba	8
Hohl Flute	8	Celeste	8
Principal	4	Gemshorn	4
Flute	4	Piccolo	2
Fifteenth	2	Tuba	8
Clarinet	8	Oboe	8
PEDAL		Tremulant	
Harmonic Bass	32		
Bourdon	16		
Bass Flute	8		

COUPLERS: unison, sub and octave
COMPASS & ACTION: not stated

But still this was not good enough and, in 1963, the organ was rebuilt yet again, this time by Henry Groves of Nottingham. Pipework was placed high up in the west gable of the nave while the console remained in the south-east chapel. In this final modification the specification was:

GREAT		SWELL	
Large Open Diapason	8	Violin diapason	8
Small Open Diapason	8	Gedacht	8
Dulciana	8	Gamba	8
Stopped Diapason	8	Celeste	8
Principal	4	Gemshorn	4
Wald Flute	4	Sesquialtera (2 ranks)	
Fifteenth	2	Cornopean	8
Trumpet	8	Oboe	8
PEDAL		Tremulant	
Sub Bass	32		
Bourdon	16		
Bass Flute	8		

COUPLERS: unison, sub and octave   ACTION: electro-pneumatic

The sorry saga came to an end in 1977 when the above instrument was finally abandoned and a new organ was built by Messrs Wood of Huddersfield. It is free-standing and is once more located in the south-east chapel, but, being of shallow modern design, the egress of sound is better than it ever could have been with the much bulkier Victorian-based instruments. It has an attractively simple, modern case with the tallest compartments of pipes cantilevered at each side. Tonally it is constructed on the unit-extension principle, giving the following quasi-Baroque stop-list derived from four basic ranks of pipes.

GREAT		SWELL	
Contra Gedackt	16	Gedackt	8
Principal	8	Principal	4
Gedackt	8	Gedackt	4
Octave	4	Nazard	2-2/3
Gedackt	4	Octave	2
Gedackt	2	Tierce	1-3/5
Mixture (3 ranks)		Larigot	1-1/3
Trumpet	8	Cymbal (2 ranks)	
PEDAL			
Sub Bass	16		
Principal	8		
Bass Flute	8		
Octave	4		
Recorder	2		
Mixture (2 ranks)			
Trumpet	16		
Octave Trumpet	4		

COUPLERS: 3 unison   ACTION: electric
COMPASS: Manuals 58; Pedal 30

The four extended ranks are: Sub Bass 16; Principal 8; Gedackt 8 (enclosed); Trumpet 16 (enclosed from 8ft). This instrument now serves its purpose efficiently and is well on the way to lasting longer than most of its predecessors.

PARISH CHURCH OF ST NICHOLAS, ALLESTREE LANE

This is a new church of simplified brick Gothic, completed in 1958, and with excellent acoustics. Its first instrument was an electronic, but this was replaced in 1970 by the 1901 Steele & Keay organ acquired from Chapel Street Methodist in Ripley. As originally built its stops were:

GREAT		SWELL	
Open Diapason	8	Open Diapason	8
Stop'd Diapason	8	Lieblich Gedact	8
Dulciana	8	Keraulophon	8
Principal	4	Voix Celeste	8
Lieblich Flute	4	Geigen Principal	4
		Oboe	8
PEDAL			
Bourdon	16		

COUPLERS: 3 unison; Swell to Great octave
COMPASS: Manuals 58; Pedal 30
ACTION: mechanical

The installation in St Nicholas was by H. Cantrill of Castle Donington. There were two stop alterations: Fifteenth 2 in place of Lieblich Flute 4, the latter going to the Swell in place of Voix Celeste 8.

In spite of helpful acoustics the organ was still limited for the large building and for the good musical tradition that had been built up. Further work was therefore carried out in 1991 by M.C. Thompson of Burton-on-Trent. The Pedal action was electrified and more manual tonal alterations were made with remarkably good effect. As well as more transposing of existing material some pipework was introduced from the de-commissioned organ at Breadsall Parish Church (qv). The stop-list now reads:

GREAT		SWELL	
Open Diapason	8	Lieblich Gedact	8
Stop'd Diapason	8	Lieblich Flute	4
Principal	4	Principal	4
Nazard	2-2/3	Fifteenth	2
Fifteenth	2	Larigot	1-1/3
		Trumpet	8
PEDAL			
Bourdon	16		

METHODIST CHURCH, DUFFIELD ROAD

The chapel with the illuminated blue Cross is a well-known feature to passers-by on the busy A6 road. Surprisingly for such a large urban area, it is the only church (other than the two Anglican ones) to possess a pipe organ. Of these three organs, however, this is the most historic, albeit much changed internally. It came from Chapel Street Methodist in Duffield (qv) in (or soon after) 1943 when that chapel closed. Its arrival in Allestree replaced a harmonium that had led the singing for nearly fifty years.

It is a four-stop chamber organ with later Pedal pipes added to the rear. The well-preserved case is of elegant Regency mahogany with dummy display pipes in the form of two side towers and a centre flat panel—all beneath a straight cornice of Classical type (though the pipe openings themselves have suggestions of "Gothick" details). The casework has been extended backwards in matching wood to hide (partially) the later Pedal pipes.

The original date of the organ is possibly c1810 and there is evidence of it having had a GG manual compass and perhaps an octave of pedals. The present specification, however, together with most of the pipework, is of a later date.

GREAT		PEDAL	
Stopped Bass (12 notes)	8	Bourdon	16
Open Diapason (Tenor-C)	8		
Dulciana (Tenor-C)	8		
Suabe Flute (Tenor-C)	8		
Principal	4		

COUPLER: Great to Pedal
COMPASS: Manual 54 (from Bass-C); Pedal 30
ACTION: mechanical

At what stage the various alterations took place is not known—more research needs to be done on this interesting old instrument. Nevertheless the potential is there and it cries out for a sympathetic restoration to something more in character with its obvious stylistic origins.

Early C19th organ from Duffield Chapel Street, now in Allestree Methodist Church

3 BREADSALL

Facing Allestree across the Derwent, Breadsall is the first village on the east bank as one goes north from present-day Derby. It is a small, unspoilt community of no more than 1,500 population. The slender fourteenth century spire forms an important landmark in this part of the valley while the body of the church contains material from both Norman and Early English periods.

The peace of the village was rudely shattered in 1913 when the church went up in flames (—some say at the hands of the Suffragettes), causing extreme damage to fabric and fittings, including the organ.

PARISH CHURCH OF ALL SAINTS

The first reference to an instrument is in the notebook of Alexander Buckingham:

> "This Organ was Made by Steven White, Cumberland Street, Fitzroy Square, London, but I think the Venetion (sic!) Swell and the Bellows have been added by Flight. It was bought at the Pantechnicon in London by the Revd. H.R. Crewe for 45 pounds and erected in Breadsall Church by A. Buckingham, 17 January 1834".

It apparently had four stops (no details given). White's 1857 Directory describes it as a "small organ" in a gallery.

In August 1889 "Musical Opinion" printed the specification of a new organ by Wadsworth & Bro of Manchester:

GREAT		SWELL	
Open Diapason	8	Lieblich Bourdon	16
Claribel & Stopt Bass	8	Open Diapason	8
Dulciana	8	Hohl Flöte	8
Gamba	8	Salicional	8
Principal	4	Voix Celestes	8
Harmonic Flute	4	Gemshorn	4
		Fagotto	8
PEDAL			
Bourdon	16		
Bass Flute	8		

COUPLERS: 3 unison; Swell octave

This is the instrument that must have been totally destroyed in the 1913 fire. Following rebuilding of the church a new organ was introduced in 1922, by J.H. Adkins of Derby. It was situated against the north wall of the chancel and its format was tall rather than deep.

1905 Kirkland organ in Little Eaton Church

GREET		SWELL	
Open Diapason	8	Violin Diapason	8
Hohl Flute	8	Lieblich Gedackt	8
Dulciana	8	Viol d'Orchestre	8
Lieblich Flute	4	Voix Celeste	8
		Salicet	4
PEDAL		Oboe	8
Bourdon	16	Tremulant	

COUPLERS: unison, sub and octave
COMPASS: Manuals 61; Pedal 30
ACTION: pneumatic

A specification such as this was obviously lacking in any appreciable brightness. Eventually, in 1962, Henry Willis & Sons of London provided a new Quartane (2 ranks) in place of the Swell Voix Celeste. Since the Swell pipework was situated above (rather than, more usually, behind) the Great Organ, the new stop added quite an "éclat" to the overall ensemble. However, by 1985 there was considerable dissatisfaction with this instrument and it was replaced by an electronic organ. Some of the pipes (including the 1962 Quartane) were used in the tonal enhancement of the organ at Allestree St Nicholas (qv).

4 LITTLE EATON

North of Breadsall the valley starts to close in. The village of Little Eaton occupies the head of a promontory between the Derwent and its tributary, the Bottle Brook, which flows in from the north east.

PARISH CHURCH OF ST PAUL

The church was built in 1791 and enlarged in 1837, but it is the "Normanization" of 1869 which is now its dominant characteristic.

The organ is in memory of the Revd Stanley Owens, Vicar from 1901 to 1903, and was built in 1905 by Alfred Kirkland of London. It has an unspoilt Romantic tonal ensemble of good musical quality, though it lacks the brightness of any stop above 4ft pitch (– one would like to think that the "prepared" slider on the Great Organ was intended for just such a stop, but its Tenor-C compass suggests more probably a Clarinet 8).

GREAT		SWELL	
Open Diapason	8	Open Diapason	8
Stopped Diapason	8	Lieblich Gedeckt	8
Gamba	8	Viol d'Orchestre	8
Dulciana	8	Vox Angelica	8
Principal	4	Gemshorn	4
Lieblich Flute	4	Cornopean	8
(prepared stop)		Oboe	8
		Tremulant	
PEDAL			
Bourdon	16		
Bass Flute	8		

COUPLERS: 3 unison
COMPASS: Manuals 56; Pedal 30
ACTION: Manuals mechanical; Pedal pneumatic

METHODIST CHURCH (former UMFC)

This small red-brick chapel was built in 1906. In 1945 an organ by Bevington
& Sons (of about the 1880's) was acquired from Swanwick Hall and erected on
a raised platform at the front. The installation was by J.H. Adkins who, six years
later, replaced the old trigger Swell pedal with a balanced one. Particularly
attractive were the stencilled front pipes and the wrought-iron strapwork on the
console lid. In 1981 the chapel closed and the following year the organ was
transferred by J.H. Poyser to the Derby Mansfield Street Methodist Church.
(*Illustration of console on page viii*).

GREAT		SWELL	
Open Diapason	8	Bell Gamba	8
Rohr Flute	8	Lieblich Gedact	8
Dulciana	8	Flute Harmonic	4
Principal	4		
Clarinet	8		

PEDAL	
Bourdon	16

COUPLERS: 3 unison; sub octave Swell
COMPASS: Manuals 56; Pedal 25
ACTION: mechanical

5   QUARNDON

*A small and attractive hill-top village with only a modest amount of modern development.
From its northern ridge it enjoys excellent views over Duffield and the valleys of the
Derwent and the lower Ecclesbourne .*

PARISH CHURCH OF ST PAUL

The church, at the summit of the village, was built in 1874 and replaces an
earlier one on a site lower down the hill, of which a mere fragment of masonry
remains.

There is more to the organ than meets the eye. It is by J.M. Grunwell of
Derby and almost certainly dates from the building of the present church,
though some of the pipes (and perhaps even the console, with its tall, vertical
columns of drawstops) may be of earlier vintage.

The Derby organ builder, Charles Eden, did some unspecified work in about
1900. In 1920 the organ was moved by J.H. Adkins from a chamber north of
the chancel to its present position at the east end of the north nave-aisle and
at this point it was known to have had the following specification:

GREAT		SWELL	
Open Diapason	8	Double Diapason	16
Stopped Diapason Bass	8	Open Diapason	8
Stopped Diapason	8	Gedact	8
Dulciana	8	Viol d'Orchestre	8
Principal	4	Voix Celeste	8
Lieblich Flute	4	Gemshorn	4
Fifteenth	2	Cornopean	8
PEDAL		Oboe	8
Bourdon	16	Tremulant	

COUPLERS: 3 unison
COMPASS: Manuals 56; Pedal 30
ACTION: Manuals mechanical; Pedal pneumatic

New casework was added to the west-facing side in 1949 as a war memorial. In 1971 H. Cantrill of Castle Donington fitted a Fifteenth in place of the Swell Voix Celeste and, at the same time, supplied replacement casework for the main south prospect of the organ. Finally, in 1991, J.H. Poyser carried out an overhaul and added a Mixture (2 ranks) in place of the Swell Oboe.

6 DUFFIELD

The mediaeval parish of Duffield was once very large, stretching some five miles up both the Derwent and the Ecclesbourne valleys, and including all of what is present-day Belper together with many of the surrounding villages.

The Parish Church occupies a Saxon site by the Derwent, close to the bridge which, from the thirteenth century until recent times, was the first crossing point north of Derby. The Ecclesbourne joins the main river in the meadows nearby; and it is on the banks of the former (rather than the Derwent) that the village has developed from Norman times onwards, leaving the church somewhat remote from the present centre of habitation.

PARISH CHURCH OF ST ALKMUND

Alexander Buckingham visited Duffield in 1824 and attended to a 5-stop organ (which he thought to be by Hancock) for Sir Charles Colvile of Duffield Hall. Although the Colviles were great benefactors of the church the probability is that this was a private instrument in the house and not one that Sir Charles had engaged Buckingham to work on in the church.

Prior to a restoration (at the expense of the Colvile family) in 1846-7 the church contained a singing gallery at the west end in which there functioned a band of instrumentalists. It is around this date that we find the first definite attribution of an organ to Duffield Church—in Sperling's notebook of c1850:

"Gray & Davison 1849   5 stops   One row of keys GG to F   General Swell"

This instrument was the gift of Mr John Balguy of Duffield Park House and is believed to have also had an optional barrel mechanism.

In January 1877 the "Derby & Chesterfield Reporter" contained a letter from a visitor who had attended Divine Service in Duffield Church and who complained that "the sound of the unharmonious organ" made him put his hands over his ears! Later that same year (perhaps as a result of the above complaint) an organ fund was raised – the most likely objective of which would have been to carry out improvements to the existing Gray & Davison (– the removal of the barrel, for example, and perhaps the addition of a second keyboard and pedals).

A further restoration of the church in 1896-7 by J.O. Scott resulted in the installation of a new organ by Nicholson & Lord of Walsall in the north-east chapel. It had tracker (ie mechanical) action and (as relayed from memory by a former Organist) a comprehensive specification typical of the best type of Romantic instrument:

1972 Cousans organ in Duffield Church

GREAT		SWELL	
Large Open Diapason	8	Bourdon	16
Small Open Diapason	8	Violin Diapason	8
Stop Diapason Bass	8	Lieblich Gedact	8
Clarabella	8	Salicional	8
Dulciana	8	Voix Celeste	8
Gamba	8	Gemshorn	4
Principal	4	Piccolo	2
Harmonic Flute	4	Mixture	
Fifteenth	2	Cornopean	8
Mixture		Oboe	8
Clarinet	8		

PEDAL	
Open Diapason	16
Violone	16
Bourdon	16
Flute	8

This was obviously an excellent instrument by a top-class late Victorian builder, though it may well have suffered from its strangulated location in a side chapel whose low-arched openings were filled in with wood panelling and wrought-iron grilles—all of which would have accounted for the next move.

In 1972, following a bequest, a new organ by Cousans of Lincoln was installed, with pipework in an elevated position at the west end and the console at the east end of the south nave-aisle. Its specification was drawn up by the Diocesan Organs Adviser, Dr. W.L. Sumner, and it incorporated pipes and parts from another, slightly smaller instrument. Unfortunately its over-assertive Mixtures result in a sound that can, at times, be too brilliant for its surroundings.

GREAT		SWELL	
Open Diapason	8	Open Diapason	8
Hohl Flute	8	Stopped Diapason	8
Dulciana	8	Salicional	8
Principal	4	Voix Celeste	8
Lieblich Flute	4	Gemshorn	4
Twelfth	2-2/3	Blockflöte	2
Fifteenth	2	Mixture (3 ranks)	
Mixture (3 ranks)		Contra Oboe	16
		Trompette	8
PEDAL		Krummhorn	4
Violone	16	Tremulant	
Bourdon	16		
Violoncello	8		
Bass Flute	8		
Choral Bass	4		

COUPLERS: unison and octave
COMPASS: Manuals 56; Pedal 30
ACTION: electro-pneumatic

In 1982 Messrs Wood of Huddersfield placed some ex-Conacher pipes (made by Zimmermann of Paris) into the Swell Open Diapason. Then in 1991, in an attempt to improve the "body" of tone, the Johnson Organ Co of Derby replaced part of the Great Open Diapason and Principal with ex-Nicholson pipes of larger scale and also provided new Trompette pipes for the Swell.

BAPTIST CHURCH

A delightful red-brick chapel of 1830, marred only by the fact that its elegant round-topped windows have lost their traditional sashes. The interior has a congregational gallery at the back and a choir one at the front in which is situated the organ.

It must have been the Parish Church's acquisition of an instrument from Nicholson & Lord that inspired the Baptists to turn to that same firm for their new organ in 1897. It cost £215, and £12-10s was received for the sale of the old one (– whatever that may have been).

GREAT		SWELL	
Open Diapason	8	Open Diapason	8
St Diap Bass		Lieblich Gedact	8
with Clala Treb (sic!)	8	Salicional	8
Dulciana	8	Gemshorn	4
Principal	4	Oboe	8
Wald Flute	4		
Fifteenth	2		

PEDAL	
Bourdon	16
Bass Flute	8

COUPLERS: 3 unison
COMPASS: Manuals 56; Pedal 30
ACTION: Manuals mechanical; Pedal pneumatic

In 1972 some tonal alterations were made by the Johnson Organ Co of Derby:

Great Wald Flute replaced by Twelfth 2-2/3
Swell Salicional replaced by Piccolo 2
New Mixture (2 ranks) added to Swell on
pneumatic action

It is a very effective organ, speaking boldly, and ideally situated in the traditional chapel gallery position.

1897 Nicholson & Lord organ in Duffield Baptist Church

TRINITY METHODIST CHURCH, KING STREET

Duffield's first Wesleyan Chapel was built in 1777 on the south side of King Street. Music was led by a band of instruments.

Mid C19th organ in former King Street Wesleyan Chapel, Duffield
(notional reconstruction by Peter Greenwood from an old photograph)

In 1843 a new chapel was built in Chapel Street (qv) and the old building became a schoolroom. Mr Gervase Cooper was appointed first Organist of the new chapel in 1844. Five years later, however, bitter strife broke out and the Chapel Street Trustees voted to secede from the main Wesleyan body, joining up before long with the newly-formed United Methodist Free Church (UMFC).

Disheartened, the handful of members (including their Organist) who wished to remain Wesleyan returned to the old King Street chapel where, before long, an organ was installed for Mr Cooper to play. An old photograph shows a small instrument of 1850's appearance with a flat, battlemented cornice to its casework. It stood in the front left corner, facing (unusually) across the pulpit area. Gervase Cooper continued to preside over this organ until his 93rd year and acquired the reputation of being "the oldest organist in Methodism"!

The present red-brick Gothic Trinity Chapel was built on the opposite side of the street in 1904, the old eighteenth century building then being sold and adapted for its current use as a Masonic Hall. For a couple of years the old organ (not to mention the even older Organist!) appears to have functioned in the new building. In 1906 Gervase Cooper died. In that same year J.H. Adkins of Derby installed a new 2-manual organ at a cost of £315, the old one being taken in part exchange.

GREAT		SWELL	
Open Diapason	8	Bourdon	16
Hohl Flute	8	Violin Diapason	8
Dulciana	8	Lieblich Gedact	8
Principal	4	Viol d'Orchestre	8
Wald Flute	4	Voix Celeste	8
Piccolo	2	Gemshorn	4
		Mixture (3 ranks)	
PEDAL		Cornopean	8
Bourdon	16	Oboe	8
Dolce	16	Tremulant	
Bass Flute	8		

COUPLERS: 3 unison
COMPASS: Manuals 61; Pedal 30
ACTION: Manual mechanical; Pedal pneumatic

The new church had an Anglican-style "chancel" with the organ chamber on the south side. The organ itself, however, did not prove very satisfactory and a number of changes were made over the years. In 1936 J.H. Adkins added to the Great a Clarinet and a Large Open Diapason – the latter with display pipes in a west-facing arch. Then, in 1978, the Johnson Organ Co fitted a new Swell soundboard, reducing it from nine speaking stops to six (8, 8, 8, 4, Mixture, Oboe); the Cornopean was revoiced as a Trumpet and transferred to the Great in place of the 1936 Clarinet.

Still none of these changes helped matters significantly. Eventually, in 1985, the organ was replaced by a smaller, more compact instrument, in a free-standing position within the main nave – basically an 1884 Forster & Andrews (from Market Drayton) but with a liberal infusion of new and substitute pipework. The installation was by E.R. Stow of Derby with volunteer helpers from the church. The result is, at last, an effective and useful musical instrument.

GREAT		SWELL	
Open Diapason	8	Rohr Gedact	8
Stopped Diapason	8	Keraulophon	8
Principal	4	Lieblich Flute	4
Gemshorn	2	Fifteenth	2
Mixture (2 ranks)		Cornopean	8

PEDAL	
Bourdon	16
Principal	8
Octave	4

COUPLERS: 3 unison
COMPASS: Manuals 56; Pedal 30
ACTION: Manuals mechanical;
    Pedal electric (independent ranks)

CHAPEL STREET METHODIST CHURCH
(former Wesleyan then UMFC)

We have seen (above) that this chapel – an elegant stone structure, still retaining all of its round-topped double-storey sash windows—was built in 1843. We have also seen that, during its brief six years of occupancy by the Wesleyans, an Organist (Gervase Cooper) was appointed in 1844. This event probably co-incided with the installation of an organ, and it is tempting to speculate that it may have been supplied by Joseph Gratian of Belper who, in that same year, built an organ for the large Wesleyan Chapel in that town. Otherwise we know nothing of the instrument left behind when the continuing Wesleyan congregation (including Mr Cooper) returned to King Street in 1849.

The first solid information is in J H Adkins' records:

"United Methodist Church Duffield   1914 June 5th
To Second Hand Pipe Organ as per specification (– not recorded!)
& agreement for Old Organ   £95-0-0"

This second-hand instrument of unknown origin is, in fact, the one that went to Allestree Methodist (qv) following closure of Chapel Street in 1943 and the final re-unification of its congregation with that of King Street.

What seems strange, though, is that Chapel Street – a substantial building with an influential congregation at the time—should in 1914 have invested in what can only be described as a chamber organ (1-manual, 6 stops), especially when their King Street "rivals" had recently acquired a 2-manual with 18 stops costing £315! It has been suggested that the answer may lie in the fact that Chapel Street had a ground-floor schoolroom in which could have been installed the little chamber organ, while the main upper chapel had a second, much larger instrument for congregational worship. This theory could be borne out by a confusing entry in the Scotchbrook notebooks in which the heading "Duffield UM" has been crossed out and replaced by "Long Eaton John-Baptist". The specification actually given under this altered heading bears no relationship with any organ at Long Eaton. One might, therefore, reasonably conclude that what we still have there is the stop-list of "Duffield UM".

GREAT		SWELL	
Open Diap.	(8)	Gedact	(8)
Stop. Diap.	(8)	Gamba	(8)
Clarabella	(8)	Vox Celeste	(8)
Dulciarna (sic!)	(8)	Harmonic Flute	(4)
PEDAL		Tremulant	
Bourdon	(16)		

COUPLERS: 3 unison; Sw super
COMPASS & ACTION: not given

Not exactly an exciting musical formula by our present standards, but in the Edwardian period such a foundational tonal scheme would have been looked on in a much more favourable light – and, given a good, open position in the chapel, it probably served its purpose perfectly adequately (– more so, perhaps, than did the larger instrument at King Street which was bedevilled by its "chancel" chamber location).

For many years the Chapel Street building was used for industrial purposes (– fortunately without any architectural harm) but, in the mid-1980's, it reverted to worship once more in the hands of the Duffield Emmanuel Community Church and it is now known as Emmanuel Christian Centre.

7 HAZELWOOD

The village is very small – little more than a crossroads with some houses and (since the nineteenth century) a church. It is on the western side of the Chevin "massif" (maximum height 625ft), which lies between the Derwent and the Ecclesbourne and which may fairly be regarded as the first area of true Pennine scenery north of Derby.

PARISH CHURCH OF ST JOHN THE EVANGELIST

The church, designed by the Derby architect, H.I. Stevens, dates from 1840, the Parish being one of those created out of the old Duffield one. Following a fire the church was restored in 1902 and this is also the date of the present organ – by C Lloyd & Co of Nottingham.

GREAT		SWELL	
Open Diapason	8	Violin Diapason	8
Dulciana	8	Salicional	8
Clarabella	8	Voix Celeste	8
Principal	4	Lieblich Flute	4
Harmonic Flute	4	Oboe	8
PEDAL			
Bourdon	16		

COUPLERS: 3 unison; Swell octave
COMPASS: Manuals 58; Pedal 30
ACTION: Manuals mechanical; Pedal pneumatic

In 1980 the Johnson Organ Co of Derby replaced the Great Harmonic Flute by a Fifteenth 2. This has certainly improved the overall brightness though the sound still finds great difficulty in getting through to the nave from its source deep in a chamber on the north side of the chancel.

8 TURNDITCH

The village is built almost entirely along the main Belper-Ashbourne road as it rises westwards from the Ecclesbourne valley.

PARISH CHURCH OF ALL SAINTS

Built as one of four chapels-of-ease in the old Duffield Parish, the church has a south door bearing the date 1630, though the original structure is believed to be considerably older. It is without tower or aisles but has a chancel that was built as an extension in 1883-4.

The organ is partly in a vestry recess on the north side of the old nave and was installed in 1891 (replacing a harmonium) – but it was not new. The lowest pallet on the Great chest bears the date 1863, and both the Great Organ pipework and the design of the casework are consistent with a 1-manual "Chancel Organ" of this period. Its appearance is somewhat reminiscent of a late mediaeval "Positive" organ of the type depicted in Van Eyck's famous altarpiece at Ghent. Bellows weights with the initials "ND" suggest that the 1891 installation may have been by Noble of Derby. It is quite possible that a short-compass Swell Organ may have been added at this time.

In 1913 the present vestry was built to accommodate J.H. Adkins' "addition" to the organ. By this we might understand the likely enlargement of a physically small, short-compass Swell to one of full compass, involving the provision of a much larger Swell box (at the rear of the organ) and, in the event, contrived by the fitting of a second-hand 61-note chest reduced to 56 notes to conform with the rest of the instrument!

Before 1986 the organ had the following stops:

GREAT			SWELL	
Open Diapason	8		Stop Diapason Swell	(8)
Stop'd Diapason Bass	(8)		Gamba	8
Claribel	(8)		Principal	4
Viol d'Amour	8		Oboe	8
Principal	(4)		Celeste	8
Fifteenth	(2)		Tremulant	

PEDAL	
Bourdon	16

COUPLERS: 3 unison
COMPASS: Manuals 56; Pedal 29
ACTION: mechanical

1863 organ in Turnditch Church

In 1986 it was overhauled by Jardine Church Organs of Manchester and some tonal alterations were made:

> Great Viol d'Amour replaced by Twelfth 2-2/3
> Swell Oboe replaced by Harmonic Flute 4
> Swell Principal 4 transposed to 2ft

The result of this was that, what had been a fairly ordinary mid-nineteenth century organ with assorted later additions, became a much more cohesive musical instrument of considerable charm and period character.

9 IDRIDGEHAY

In this survey we follow the detour of the Ecclesbourne valley since, by virtue of the large mediaeval parishes of Duffield and Wirksworth, it is very much linked with the Derwent and, in fact, provides an alternative, parallel route between Duffield and Cromford—and it is about half way along this route that we pass through the small community of Idridgehay.

PARISH CHURCH OF ST JAMES

Idridgehay acquired Parish status on the completion and consecration of its tiny church (– a truly "multum in parvo" design by Stevens) in 1855.

The organ is by Bevington & Sons and is one of that firm's model "Chancel Organs". No date is given, but such instruments (by a number of different builders) were popularized for a decade or so following the 1862 International Exhibition: they fulfilled a need at a time when robed choirs were increasingly being established – even in the smallest churches.

GREAT		
Bourdon	(16)	13 notes
Open Diapason	(8)	
Stop'd Bass	(8)	12 notes
Claribel	(8)	Tenor-C
Dulciana	(8)	Tenor-C
Principal	(4)	
Flute Harmonic	(4)	Tenor-C

PEDAL – permanently coupled (no stops)

> COMPASS: Manual 54; Pedal 25
> ACTION: mechanical
> All stops enclosed in a swell except Bourdon and
>   Open Diapason

The pipework is not in a chamber but is against the north wall of the chancel, cantilevered forward over the console. The tone is pleasant and unforced.

10 KIRK IRETON

A mediaeval parish to the west of the Ecclesbourne valley. The village has a number of substantial stone houses dating back to the seventeenth and eighteenth centuries, while the church itself is of Norman origin.

PARISH CHURCH OF HOLY TRINITY

The "Derby Mercury" of 3rd August, 1859, reported a new organ in this church. It was a Chancel Organ of the "St Cecilia" range produced by the great Henry Willis.

GREAT

Open Diapason	(8)
Dulciana	(8)
Principal	(4)
Fifteenth	(2)

COMPASS: Manual 54
ACTION: mechanical

Consistent with the desire, later in the century, to increase the size of organs, alterations have inevitably occurred. At the church restoration of 1873-4 the old west gallery (probably containing the organ) was removed. Then in 1891 the sum of £200 was spent on the "restoration" of the organ by Alfred Kirkland of London. Bearing in mind that the Willis "St Cecilia" would have cost less than half this, the substantial sum can only imply that this is the point at which pedals and a second manual keyboard were added.

Further work was done by J.H. Adkins in the early part of the twentieth century and by Henry Willis & Sons in 1966, by which time the state of the organ was:

GREAT		SWELL	
Open Diapason	8	Gamba	8
Dulciana	8	Flute Metal	8
Principal	4	Voix Celeste	8
Lieblich Flute	4	Gemshorn	4
PEDAL		Oboe	8
Bourdon	16	Tremulant	

COUPLERS: 3 unison
COMPASS: Manuals 56; Pedal 30
ACTION: mechanical

In 1992 an overhaul was carried out by the Johnson Organ Co of Derby in which the Great Organ was restored to its former Willis specification (see above). The displaced Lieblich Flute was put on the Swell in place of the Oboe and the Gemshorn was transposed to become Salicetina 2. The consequence of these alterations is that (as at Turnditch) the instrument has had restored to it an overall tonal scheme and sonority more in keeping with its early Victorian character.

11 WIRKSWORTH

Situated in a bowl at the head of the Ecclesbourne valley, Wirksworth has been a centre of lead mining from Roman and Saxon times. With the eventual decline of this industry in the nineteenth century there started to rise the limestone quarrying which now forms such an impressively disfiguring backdrop to the otherwise charming present-day market town.

PARISH CHURCH OF ST MARY

St Mary's is a large, cruciform church standing within a cathedral-like close of old houses which surround the large churchyard.

The heraldic Calendar of Patent Rolls, 1503, makes mention of William and Nicholas Stroke, organ makers of "Wyrkesworth", Derbyshire. They are the only builders native to the County that we know of before the nineteenth century and it is not surprising that it should be Wirksworth, with its devotion to lead (an important ingredient in organ building), where we should find them. Nothing else is known about the Strokes, though one might safely guess that "ij payre of organes", mentioned by Edward VI's Commissioners in 1547 as being in Wirksworth Church, would be one of their products. It is most unlikely, however, that such an instrument would have survived the anti-organ attitudes of the later Elizabethan and also the Commonwealth reformers.

Nearly three centuries later, in 1826, a 2-manual organ with 11 stops (no details) and a 12-note pedalboard was built by Elliot & Hill of London in a choir gallery under the central tower – a situation that was soon to be found "objectionable". In 1853 it was removed by Buckingham ("father and son") to a platform at the west end of the nave and in 1856 William Hill (by now on his own) added a new Swell and some Pedal pipes of 16ft.

1861 saw further changes. The organ was rebuilt by Forster & Andrews of Hull and enlarged to 17 stops, with Great and Swell compasses converted to Bass-C and Tenor-C respectively and with a 29-note pedalboard.

These alterations met with approval, but within very few years the church building was found to be in urgent need of major restoration – an operation that was to be supervised by G.G. Scott in 1870-6, in the course of which the organ was moved to a position north of the present choirstalls in accordance with later nineteenth century theories that "the conveniences as well as the proprieties of worship" demanded that the Choir should be in the chancel.

By the 1890's an organ with "noisy" tracker action, no registration aids and only 17 stops was clearly no longer regarded as adequate for St Mary's. Consequently the old organ was swept away and a totally new instrument by Brindley & Foster of Sheffield was installed in 1899. Like its immediate predecessor it was placed in the transept aisle, north of the choirstalls. It had Brindley's latest type of pneumatic action (employing sliderless chests) and an elegant console with the firm's characteristically large, porcelain-headed stop-knobs.

GREAT		SWELL	
Bourdon	16	Lieblich Bourdon	16
Large Open Diapason	8	Geigen Principal	8
Small Open Diapason	8	Rohr Gedackt	8
Claribel	8	Viol da Gamba	8
Principal	4	Voix Celeste	8
Harmonic Flute	4	Octave	4
Grave Mixture (2 ranks)		Full Mixture (3 ranks)	
Posaune	8	Cornopean	8
		Oboe	8
		Tremulant	
CHOIR		PEDAL	
Gedackt	8	Major Bass	16
Dulciana	8	Sub Bass	16
Flute	4	Principal Bass	8
Piccolo	2	Flute Bass	8
Clarinet	8		

COUPLERS: unison, sub and octave
COMPASS: Manuals 58; Pedal 30
ACTION: pneumatic

A splendid instrument, but one whose problem was always its action – good while it lasted, but almost impossible to maintain. In 1955 it was electrified by Kingsgate Davidson of London but this did not prevent its eventual failure by the mid-1980's. In 1987, following a Consistory Court, the organ was replaced by an electronic one and the parts were sold to an organ builder in Bath.

BAPTIST CHURCH

Records show that an organ (believed to have been originally of one manual) was overhauled by J.H. Adkins in 1906 and that the same firm rebuilt the instrument in 1919.

GREAT		SWELL	
Open Diapason	8	Geigen Principal	8
Small Open Diapason	8	Stop Diapason	8
Stop Diapason	8	Viol d'Orchestre	8
Dulciana	8	Voix Celeste	8
Principal	4	Principal	4
Flute	4	Cornopean	8
Fifteenth	2	Oboe	8
PEDAL		Tremulant	
Bourdon	16		

COUPLERS: 3 unison; Swell sub octave
COMPASS: not given by Scotchbrook
ACTION: Manuals mechanical; Pedal pneumatic

This organ was replaced by an electronic in 1988.

EBENEZER METHODIST CHURCH, CHAPEL LANE
(former Wesleyan)
Scotchbrook gives the specification of a small organ by J.H. Adkins of Derby.

GREAT		SWELL	
Open Diapason	8	Violin Diapason	8
Dulciana	8	Lieblich Gedact	8
Flute	4	Viol d'Orchestre	8
		Oboe	8
PEDAL		Tremulant	
Bourdon	16		

COUPLERS: 3 unison; Swell octave
COMPASS & ACTION: not stated

The chapel itself, dating from 1810, was closed in 1961 and demolished in 1983.

BOLEHILL METHODIST CHURCH (former Primitive)

Though part of Wirksworth, the little hillside community of Bolehill has the feel of a small village in its own right – a characteristic emphasized by its isolation from major through-roads. The chapel stands in a commanding position at the top of a sloping space that was formerly the Green: the view over Wirksworth and the Ecclesbourne is superb.

The original chapel of 1823 is now the schoolroom. Joined to the front of it, on the steeply sloping site, is the present 1852 building – a classic chapel with real atmosphere, having an elegant rear balcony (with clock) and two storeys of Georgian round-topped sash windows.

The organ fits somewhat uncomfortably on the floor to the right of the pulpit. Musically, though, it is one of those instruments that is wholly effective in its particular environment. The lack of an Open Diapason on the Great Organ is most unusual for its period – one might even say welcome, as it allows the full ensemble to be carried by the bold-sounding Gemshorn (– a Principal in all but name). One's only wish, in view of the duplication of 4ft Flutes, might be to convert the Great one to 2ft pitch: the organ really would sparkle then!

No date or nameplate is evident. A reasonable guess for it would be around 1880.

GREAT		SWELL	
Clarabella	8	Open Diapason	8
Gemshorn	4	Viol d'Amour	8
Flute	4	Harmonic Flute	4
PEDAL			
Bourdon	16		

COUPLERS: 3 unison
COMPASS: Manuals 56; Pedal 30
ACTION: mechanical

RC CHURCH OF OUR LADY & ST TERESA OF LISIEUX

A delightful little country church, surrounded by its own extensive graveyard and situated on the slope of a wooded hill. It dates from 1931 and was built as the result of a benefaction. Close by is the nineteenth century Providence Mill and a cluster of old cottages which form the little community of Gorsey Bank, less than a mile south-east of Wirksworth town centre.

The organ is by Cousans of Lincoln – one of their "Premier" positive organs of the 1970's period. It was acquired in the mid-1980's from the RC church in Newark.

GREAT

Stop Diapason	8
Gemshorn	4
Fifteenth	2
Sifflöte	1

COMPASS: Manual 58
ACTION: mechanical

Following installation in Wirksworth the Sifflöte was transposed to 4ft pitch in order to provide a softer combination of stops for use in the quieter moments of the service: the stop label, however, remains unchanged.

UNITED REFORMED CHURCH (former Congregational)

The chapel was built in 1873, replacing an earlier one of about 1700. It has an imposing facade in Early English lancet style which, together with the apparently disproportionate loftiness of the interior, suggests that a considerably more extensive building may originally have been planned. Where one might have expected to find an organ recess behind the pulpit there is just a plain wall, against each side of which the elegant iron balcony finishes abruptly. One important effect of its great height is that the church possesses superb acoustics.

The organ is in the rear part of the U-shaped balcony, off-centre to avoid the main "west" window. It bears the label "J.M. Grunwell, Organ Builder, Derby, 1877" and is the sort of gem one always lives in hope of discovering. The specification makes one realize how much more effective it is to concentrate a complete chorus ensemble on one manual than to disperse a less-than-adequate number of stops over two keyboards. It was restored by T.W. Fearn of London in the early 1990's.

GREAT

Open Diapason	8
Stop Diapason (Bass)	8
Stop Treble	8★
Dulciana	8★
Principal	4★
Flute	4★
Twelfth	2-2/3★
Fifteenth	2★
Oboe	8★

PEDAL
Bourdon   16

COUPLER: "Keys to Pedals"
COMPASS: Manual 56; Pedal 25
ACTION: mechanical
* stops enclosed in swell

1877 Grunwell organ in Wirksworth United Reformed Church

12 MIDDLETON-BY-WIRKSWORTH

Situated high above Wirksworth and the head of the Ecclesbourne, this former lead-mining and now limestone-quarrying community has a clear identity of its own. This is highlighted by the fact that, with a population of less than a thousand, it boasts no fewer than four functioning places of worship.

PARISH CHURCH OF HOLY TRINITY

Dating from 1838, this is a simple, chapel-like structure, executed in Perpendicular Gothic style. Like many hillside chapels it makes good use of the sloping site by having schoolrooms underneath.

The church was reseated in 1885 and this could well be the date of the organ – an instrument by C. Lloyd & Co of Nottingham, situated in the north-east corner, facing the congregation (– there is no architectural chancel as such). It is a pleasantly effective instrument, still in the classical tradition, with stops up to 2ft pitch on each manual. However, it is now so badly seized up that, in order to avoid further damage to the action, it has been "moth-balled" until funds are available for restoration. (It is perhaps worth pointing out, as something of a cautionary tale, that the gift of a screen in 1925 rendered totally inaccessible the interior of the instrument, thus preventing the normal routine maintenance—other than tuning—that would probably have kept it in reasonable working order!)

GREAT		SWELL	
Open Diapason	8	Stop Diapason	8
Stopd Diapason Bass	8	Keraulophon	8
Stopd Diapason Treble	8	Gemshorn	4
Dulciana	8	Piccolo	2
Principal	4	Oboe	8
Flute	4	Tremulant	
Fifteenth	2		

PEDAL	
Grand Bourdon	16

COUPLERS: 2 unison
COMPASS: Manuals 56; Pedal 30
ACTION: mechanical

CONGREGATIONAL CHURCH

The chapel, though altered in the nineteenth century, dates from 1786 and is the earliest of Middleton's places of worship. An elegant "Gothick" arch behind the pulpit opens into a recess in which is placed the organ – another by C. Lloyd & Co, and of similar age and range to that in Holy Trinity. In 1906 J.H. Adkins effected "Removal, re-erection, cleaning, renovating, raising pressure & revoicing". The following year they added twelve Oboe pipes to complete the compass of what had been a Tenor-C rank. It has been well maintained and is a fine instrument enjoying excellent acoustics.

GREAT		SWELL	
Open Diapason	8	Stop Diapason	8
Stop Bass	8	Gamba	8
Clarabella	8	Gemshorn	4
Dulciana	8	Piccolo	2
Principal	4	Oboe	8
Flute	4	Tremulant	
Fifteenth	2		

PEDAL	
Bourdon	16

COUPLERS: 3 unison
COMPASS: Manuals 56; Pedal 30
ACTION: mechanical

METHODIST CHURCH, MAIN STREET (former Wesleyan)

This chapel, not many yards further up the street from the Parish Church, is of similar siting and external proportions, though its style is late Georgian rather than Gothic. The interior has galleries at sides and back but their classic charm is now spoiled by having heat-conserving polythene strung across them.

The rebuilding of the chapel in 1874 suggests a probable date for the organ – by Noble & Co of Derby. In 1911 it was overhauled by J.H. Adkins who added a Voix Celeste on pneumatic action as well as a Tremulant.

GREAT		SWELL	
Open Diapason	8	Gedact	8
Clarabella Flute	8	Gamba	8
Dulciana	8	Voix Celeste	8
Principal	4	Gemshorn	4
		Oboe	8
PEDAL		Tremulant	
Bourdon	16		

COUPLERS: 3 unison
COMPASS: Manuals 58; Pedal 30
ACTION: Manuals mechanical; Pedal pneumatic

MOUNT ZION METHODIST CHURCH (former Primitive)

An appropriate name for a chapel at the summit of a steeply rising village street! It is a stone building of 1906 and a good example of Methodist Gothic of the period.

The organ, in its present form, is by Beverley & Williams of Stockport (though the Great Organ is thought to be older than the rest). It is in the front right hand corner and is clothed in an opulent pine case which matches the pulpit. Installation cannot have been much after 1906, though a very early photograph apparently shows "a small organ" (– the present Great?) in the centre of the choir recess behind the pulpit.

GREAT		SWELL	
Open Diapason	(8)	Open Diapason	(8)
Clarabella	(8)	Stop Diapason	(8)
Dulciana	(8)	Gemshorn	(4)
Principal	(4)	Oboe	(8)
Fifteenth	(2)	Tremulant	

PEDAL
Bourdon   (16)

COUPLERS: 3 unison
COMPASS: Manuals 56; Pedal 30
ACTION: Manuals mechanical; Pedal pneumatic

13   HOLBROOK

Holbrook village is on the ridge east of the Derwent, opposite the lower end of the Chevin.

PARISH CHURCH OF ST MICHAEL

Originally within the parish of Duffield, a small classical church was built in 1761, becoming a parochial centre in its own right about a hundred years later. This building was enlarged in 1841 and then restored in 1887. Further extensive rebuilding took place in 1907-8 following a fire.

W. Hill & Son of London built a 1-manual organ in 1871 with the following stops:

GREAT	
Open Diapason	(8)
Dulciana	(8)
Lieblich Gedact	(8)
Principal	(4)
Wald Flute	(4)
Fifteenth	(2)

PEDAL (29 Notes)
Bourdon   (16)

ACTION: mechanical

A Swell of later nineteenth century type (probably dating from the 1887 church restoration) substantially survived the fire to be incorporated into the existing 1908 J.H. Adkins organ.

GREAT		SWELL	
Open Diapason	8	Violin Diapason	8
Dulciana	8	Lieblich Gedeckt	8
Hohl Flöte	8	Viol d'Orchestre	8
Harmonic Flute	4	Voix Celeste	8
Clarinet	8	Principal	4
PEDAL		Piccolo	2
Bourdon	16	Hautboy	8
Bass Flute	8	Tremulant	

COUPLERS: 3 unison; Swell suboctave
COMPASS: Manuals 56; Pedal 30
ACTION: Manuals mechanical; Pedal pneumatic

In 1990 J H Poyser of Derby overhauled the organ and made the following tonal alterations to improve the limited chorus of the Adkins Great Organ: Harmonic Flute and Clarinet replaced by Principal 4 and Fifteenth 2, the Harmonic Flute being transferred to the Swell in place of the Celeste. This operation was followed in 1994 by the fitting of a Cornopean 8 in place of the Hautboy. (The pipes of the Cornopean are believed to have come, by round-about means, from the Brindley & Foster organ that once stood in Belper Public Hall [qv]).

HOLBROOK MOOR METHODIST CHURCH (former UMFC)

This little chapel bears the date 1883. The organ, though, is much older and is an unspoilt historical gem. Standing at the front left, on a raised choir platform, it has casework consisting of three flush "towers" of taller pipes with "flats" (panels of smaller pipes) in between. With its projecting 2-manual console it is somewhat suggestive of the work of the important early Victorian builder, J C Bishop.

The Chapel Society Minutes show that the acquisition of an organ was approved in 1883. The instrument itself, however, is of that interesting 1840/50 type in which the Swell Organ has stops of Tenor-C compass but its keyboard has a bottom octave permanently coupled to the Great Organ.

Its origins are unknown, but some paper packing at the rear of the Swell box was discovered to bear the date 1856 and to originate from the Manchester area. The only major work since installation has been the addition by J.H. Adkins (on a pneumatic chest) of an octave of bass pipes to the one-time Tenor-C Open Diapason of the Great Organ; also the addition of a Tremulant and, in 1947, an electric blower.

GREAT		SWELL (Tenor-C:	
Open Diapason	(8)	Bass coupled to Great)	
Stop Diapason Bass	(8)	Open Diapason	(8)
Stop Diapason Treble	(8)	Stop Diapson	(8)
Dulciana	(8)	Principal	(4)
Flute	(4)	Fifteenth	(2)
Principal	(4)	Hautboy	(8)
Twelfth	(2-2/3)	Tremulant	
Fifteenth	(2)		

PEDAL
Bourdon   (16)

  COUPLERS: "Couplet" (Sw to Gt); "Pedals" (Gt to Ped)
  COMPASS: Manuals 54; Pedal 29
  ACTION: mechanical

Mid C19th organ in Holbrook Moor Methodist Church

14 MILFORD

Milford is a product of the late eighteenth century industrial era: a model mill-village squeezed into a gorge of the Derwent, with the Chevin rising steeply on its west side and a quarried gritstone cliff-face to the east.

The mill and its associated village were founded in 1780 by Jedediah Strutt of Belper. Whilst the mill itself has now mostly disappeared, the attractive terraces of stone cottages lining the hillside still remain. Though even now only having a population of less than a thousand, the village is remarkable in having built (during the nineteenth century) a church and four chapels. In 1795 a toll-bridge was constructed to carry the new turnpike road that is now the A6.

PARISH CHURCH OF HOLY TRINITY

Built in 1848, this is an "Early English" style church, clinging to a narrow site on the steep eastern slope. Earliest reference to an organ is in Bevington's list of *c* 1885 (no details), while Bulmer's 1895 Directory describes the west end as being "crossed by a gallery in which are the organ and choir seats".

In 1905 a substantial 2-manual organ by Bevington & Sons was installed in a new, purpose-built chamber to the north of the chancel. The two arched openings were fronted with attractive twin Gothic cases. For all its size, though, the instrument suffered from two major handicaps: the sound did not get out into the nave, and the tracker mechanism was quite the heaviest imaginable – both of which things were a pity, since the pipework was good and would certainly have benefited from improved action and location.

GREAT		SWELL	
Open Diapason	8	Open Diapason	8
Violin Diapason	8	Stop'd Diapason	8
Dulciana	8	Salicional	8
Flauto Traverso	8	Voix Celeste	8
Principal	4	Principal	4
Lieblich Flöte	4	Mixture (3 ranks)	
Fifteenth	2	Cornopean	8
PEDAL		Oboe	8
Bourdon	16		
Flute Bass	8		

COUPLERS: 3 unison; Swell sub octave
COMPASS: Manuals 56; Pedal 30
ACTION: Manuals mechanical; Pedal pneumatic

(Note that at the time of writing this instrument is still in the church awaiting disposal)

In 1994 the decision was taken, on account of the above-mentioned handicaps and the cost of eliminating them, to install another organ – the 1874 Grunwell at one time in Belper Baptist Church (qv). The work has been done by E R Stow of Derby (helped by local volunteers) and the opportunity has been taken to place it in a good, open position on the north side of the nave (facing south) and to modify the specification slightly from that which it had while serving temporarily in Belper St Peter's (qv). (*Illustration on page ii*)

Twin cases of 1905 Bevington organ in Milford Church

GREAT		SWELL	
Open Diapason	8	Gedact	8
Stopt Diapason	8	Spitz Flute	4
Principal	4	Mixture (2 ranks)	
Fifteenth	2		
CHOIR		PEDAL	
Lieblich Gedact	8	Sub Bass	16
Gamba	8	Gamba	8
Flute	4		
Gemshorn	2		

COUPLERS: 5 unison
COMPASS: Manuals 58; Pedal 30
ACTION: mechanical

BAPTIST CHURCH

This tiny chapel, dating from 1849, nowadays boasts a reed organ. Adkins' records, however, have entries suggestive of a pipe organ at one time:

1907: "Renovating, cleaning & repairs, £6"
1909: "To taking down Organ & removing, 12s 6d"

Perhaps the instrument in question was proving too costly to maintain!

CHEVIN ROAD METHODIST CHURCH (former Wesleyan)

A square, galleried chapel, built in 1842 and now used as a warehouse. It had a small 8-stop, 2-manual tracker organ which, according to local tradition, came from West Bridgford and was installed at Chevin Road in 1934 by J H Adkins. Following closure of the chapel it was in 1949 transferred to Ambergate Methodist (qv).

EBENEZER METHODIST CHURCH (former UMFC)

Built in 1859 and closed in 1983, this building has now been converted into holiday flats.

By the late 1870's the chapel's band of instruments was proving unreliable and so a harmonium was bought from the proceeds of the sale of the "Big Bass". Soon after, in 1881, a pipe organ was obtained from Eyam Parish Church, but this obviously proved inadequate as another exchange was effected in 1888, the builder involved being Noble of Derby. This instrument ("about forty years old") was further rebuilt and improved in 1893, at which time it was given a full-compass Pedal with Bourdon. Following a gas explosion, repairs (and possibly the addition of the Swell) were carried out in 1901 by Charles Eden of Derby (whose nameplate the organ latterly bore).

The Great Organ soundboard had originally been of GG compass and its stops had the characteristics of a pre-1850 instrument: "Treble" ranks starting at Middle-C (rather than the Victorian Tenor-C), elegant cursive script on the stop-heads and an unforced, chamber-like quality of tone. When the Swell was added at a later date an attempt was made to match the script of the Great stops. After closure of the chapel in 1983 the pipework was dispersed and used elsewhere – notably in the Davis chamber organ at the Queen's Hall Methodist Mission in Derby and the Stow chest organ normally resident in Derby Cathedral. Final specification of the Ebenezer organ before closure was:

GREAT		SWELL	
Open Diapason	8	Gamba (Tenor-C)	8
Stop Diapason Bass		Viol	8
(24 notes)	(8)	Gemshorn 8 (sic!) (– really 4)	
Stop Diapason Treble		Oboe (Tenor-C)	8
(Middle-C)	(8)	Tremulant	
Dulciana (Middle-C)	(8)		
Flute (Middle-C)	(4)		
Principal	(4)		
Fifteenth	(2)		

PEDAL	
Bourdon	16

COUPLERS: 2 unison
COMPASS: Manuals 54; Pedal 30
ACTION: mechanical

SHAW LANE METHODIST CHURCH (former Primitive)

Dating from 1823, this is the one survivor of the original three Methodist chapels in the village. An organ certainly existed here in the early 1900's since reference is made to "tuning, etc" in the Adkins records of that period.

The present organ was installed in 1933 by J.H. Adkins and came from the former Derwent Street Congregational Church in Derby. It is an instrument that could possibly have started life as a 1-manual (– the present Swell Organ), though it had certainly achieved its present specification by the 1920's (before its arrival in Milford). The only alteration at its installation was the addition of a Tremulant and of an electric blower. In 1968 the Johnson Organ Co fitted a balanced swell pedal. It remains a most effective instrument, well-placed in its front gallery position behind the pulpit.

GREAT		SWELL	
Open Diapason	8	Stopped Diapason Bass	8
Dulciana	8	Keraulophon	8
Wald Flute	8	Gamba	8
Principal	4	Dulciana Principal	4
		Fifteenth	2
PEDAL		Oboe	8
Bourdon	16		

Tremulant (to whole organ)
COUPLERS: "Manual Coupler";
  Great to Pedal (no label)
COMPASS: Manuals 56; Pedal 29
ACTION: mechanical

Shaw Lane Methodist Chapel, Milford, showing organ from Derwent Street Congregational, Derby (drawing by Peter Greenwood)

15 BELPER

From being a mere chapelry within the mediaeval parish of Duffield, Belper rose under Jedediah Strutt's mill régime to become, in the early nineteenth century, the second largest town in Derbyshire. Recognition of this fact was duly accorded by the construction in 1824 of the large church of St Peter and its subsequent elevation to parochial status. This was followed in 1850 by the creation of a second parish – that of Christ Church.

CHAPEL OF ST JOHN THE BAPTIST

The thirteenth century chapel was never able to accommodate more than about two hundred people. In 1806 a west gallery was erected and it is known that there was at this time a regular choir. Clues about an organ, however, are nebulous. Sperling's notebook of c1850 records a 1754 Snetzler organ in "Belper Church" – which, by that date, would imply the new St Peter's (though the instrument could conceivably have once stood in St John's). A report in the "Derby Mercury" of 8th October, 1818, refers to a "new" organ by Joseph Gratian of Belper in the "Established Church"–ie St John's (and opened by the builder's 10-year old daughter!). In local-press parlance then (as now) a "new" organ could imply anything from a second-hand transfer or rebuild to a totally new creation. In this instance a transfer from elsewhere would seem the most plausible interpretation. The sequence of events would therefore seem to be:

1818 Installation in St John's (by Gratian) of 1754 Snetzler
(of unknown origin)
1824 Transfer of above organ (by Gratian?) to newly completed
St Peter's Church.

The specification of this organ, as given by Sperling in c1850, was:

"Snetzler, 1754. GG short octaves to D in alt., one row of keys"

Open Diapason	(8)
Stopped Diapason	
bass & treble	(8)
Principal	(4)
Fifteenth	(2)
Sesquialtra V bass	
Cornet V treble	
Trumpet	(8)

PARISH CHURCH OF ST PETER

St Peter's, dating from 1824, is a large Perpendicular Gothic building of the
"Commissioners' " type, with a shallow chancel and commodious galleries at
sides and back. With a specified capacity of 1,800 it clearly needed more than
could be offered by the small 1754 Snetzler presumed to have been transferred
from St John's Chapel. In May 1853 it was reported locally that "the
opportunity had just presented itself" to Heage Church (qv) "of obtaining from
a neighbouring Township an excellent instrument at a moderate price". This
can only be referring to the above-mentioned Snetzler organ, for it was in
December of that same year that the new organ by Holt of Bradford was opened
in St Peter's at a service led by the Choir of Leeds Parish Church.

GREAT		SWELL (Tenor-C)	
Double Diapason		Double Diapason	(16)
(added 1855)	(16)	Open Diapason	(8)
Open Diapason	(8)	Principal	(4)
Stop Diapason (Bass)	(8)	Fifteenth	(2)
Clarabella	(8)	Fifteenth Octave Higher	
Viol de Gamba	(8)	(sic!)	(1)
Principal	(4)	Cornopean	(8)
Flute	(4)		
Twelfth	(2-2/3)		
Fifteenth	(2)		
Sesquialtra (3 ranks)			
Trumpet	(8)		

PEDAL	
Open Diapason	(16)

COUPLERS: Swell to Great; Pedals to Great (sic!)
COMPASS: Manuals 54; Pedal 27
ACTION: mechanical

The first thing one notices is that the Swell Organ lacked a Stopped Diapason and Oboe but included the unusual (and oddly named) stop of 1ft pitch. The composition of the Great Sesquialtra was also noteworthy: 19-22 for the first 25 notes; 8-15-17 for the next 24 (ie from Middle-C sharp); 8-15 for the top 5 notes.

The Gothic casework, which survives intact (though extended to the rear), has a large central "flat" with a battlemented cornice and twin arched openings containing the ten largest Open Diapason pipes of the Great Organ. Between this and the projecting corner turrets of pipes are smaller arches with, instead of pipes, wooden, lozenge-patterned grilles.

1853 Holt organ in St Peter's, Belper, showing 1873 console (print by W. Attenborough)

In 1873 the organ was rebuilt by Radcliffe & Sagar of Leeds. To bring it more in line with current fashion the Sesquialtra had its 17th rank removed while the Swell Organ was rebuilt with a new, full-compass chest and a total of seven stops (the 2ft and 1ft being re-organized as an orthodox Mixture of two ranks). Furthermore a Choir Organ was added to the rear of the Swell while the Pedal Organ was converted to pneumatic action to give an additional Bourdon. It is interesting to note that, during this operation, the signature of James J. Binns (at the time an employee of Radcliffe & Sagar, but later to branch out in a big way on his own) was pencilled inside the swell box. A specification noted by the Incumbent in 1887 gives us the state of the Radcliffe & Sagar instrument:

GREAT		SWELL	
Double Diapason	(16)	Double Diapason	(16)
Open Diapason	(8)	Open Diapason	(8)
Stopt Diapason Bass	(8)	Stopt Diapason	(8)
Clarabella Treble	(8)	Principal	(4)
Viol de Gamba	(8)	Mixture (2 ranks)	
Principal	(4)	Cornopean	(8)
Flute	(4)	Oboe	(8)
Twelfth	(2-2/3)		
Fifteenth	(2)		
Sesquialtra (2 ranks)			
Trumpet	(8)		
CHOIR		PEDAL	
Lieblich Gedact	(8)	Open Diapason	(16)
Dulciana	(8)	Bourdon	(16)
Flute	(4)		
Clarionet	(8)		

COUPLERS: 5 unison
COMPASS: Manuals 54; Pedal 29
ACTION: Manuals mechanical; Pedal pneumatic

(The use of the word "Stopt" as opposed to "Stop" is presumably an understandable slip of the pen)

In 1902 there was a "restoration" of the organ by J.H. Adkins which seems to have been largely cosmetic – including the "relettering" of stop-knobs. No changes appear to have been made to the pipework though certain stops acquired new names: Viol de Gamba became Keraulophon, Sesquialtra became Mixture and Lieblich Gedact became another Stop Diapason.

It was in this latter state that, in 1938, the Holt organ was decommissioned in favour of one of the early Hammond electronics. Forty years later, with the Hammond beginning to ail, thoughts again turned to the derelict pipe organ which had (most fortunately) been left "in situ" but was now regarded in certain circles as no more than a write-off.

There were some, however, who recognized the true value of this priceless relic. As a result a volunteer restoration project was launched under the direction of Mr. E.R. Stow of Derby, in which the main criterion was to recreate the Holt sound within the existing Radcliffe & Sagar layout and mechanism. To achieve this end the Sesquialtera (– note revised spelling) was restored to its original composition with the all-important 17th rank, while the Swell Mixture was re-arranged as a "Doublette" containing (combined) the once-more-complete 2ft and 1ft ranks. The Choir Organ received a Flageolet in place of the Dulciana and the Viol de Gamba was returned to its original name.

This work was completed in 1979 and the instrument soon established itself as a splendid example of that important genre, the Early Victorian Organ. Services, concerts, lessons, broadcasts and regular practice ensured that it was used almost daily.

1992 saw a professional continuation of the restoration process, together with (in the light of thirteen years of very intensive use) some modifications that were considered necessary to cope with the now more congregational style of worship. Messrs Wood of Huddersfield renewed both the Choir trackers and the Pedal pneumatics–the latter now being expanded to include a third stop. To provide tonal "relief" from the recently restored, highly colourful Sesquialtera an extra Mixture was added to the Great Organ in place of the Viol de Gamba. As a bonus it was also found to be possible to divide the 1979 Swell Doublette into its constituent (1853-style) 2ft and 1ft ranks.

GREAT		SWELL	
Double Diapason	(16)	Double Diapason	(16)
Open Diapason	(8)	Open Diapason	(8)
Stop Diapason Bass	(8)	Stop Diapason	(8)
Clarabella Treble	(8)	Principal	(4)
Principal	(4)	Fifteenth	(2)
Flute	(4)	Twenty Second	(1)
Twelfth	(2-2/3)	Cornopean	(8)
Fifteenth	(2)	Oboe	(8)
Mixture (3 ranks)			
Sesquialtera (3 ranks)			
Trumpet	(8)		
CHOIR		PEDAL	
Stop Diapason	(8)	Open Diapason	(16)
Flute	(4)	Bourdon	(16)
Flageolet	(2)	Trombone	(16)
Clarionette	(8)		

COUPLERS: 5 unison
COMPASS: Manuals 54; Pedal 30
ACTION: Manuals mechanical; Pedal pneumatic

While one naturally regrets the absence of the 1853 Viol de Gamba (–still in safe-keeping!) there can be no doubt that the recent modifications have greatly increased the usefulness of the organ without compromising its strongly surviving 1853/1873 personality.

THE TEMPORARY ORGAN

During the restoration of the Holt organ in 1991-2 a compact 3-manual tracker instrument by Grunwell of Derby (1874) was installed under the north gallery by E R Stow. It had once been the residence organ of T B Mellor, an Organist of St Peter's. Subsequently it was in Belper Baptist Church (qv), from where it had recently been removed and stored.

While in St Peter's it had the following stops:

GREAT		SWELL	
Open Diapason	8	Gedact	8
Stopt Diapason	8	Wald Flute	4
Principal	4	Sesquialtera (2 ranks)	
Fifteenth	2		
CHOIR		PEDAL	
Lieblich Gedact	8	Sub Bass	16
Gamba	8	Gamba	8
Flute	4		
Gemshorn	2		

COUPLERS: 5 unison
COMPASS: Manuals 58; Pedal 30
ACTION: mechanical

After completion of the main organ in 1992 the Grunwell was transferred (also on a temporary basis) to the Queen's Hall Methodist Mission in Derby which had just been rebuilt following a fire and was still awaiting construction of its replacement organ. Here the opportunity was taken to convert it to concert pitch from what had formerly been a semitone sharp (– the latter perhaps having been a measure of economy both in space and cost for what had been built as a house organ).

In 1994 this organ was moved yet again (– hopefully for the last time!) to Milford Parish Church (qv) as a permanent replacement for the Bevington instrument.

PARISH CHURCH OF CHRIST CHURCH

Built in 1850 to a design by H.I. Stevens of Derby, it is a large, aisleless hall without architectural division at the chancel or sanctuary, and is endowed with superb acoustics.

White's 1857 Directory refers to "an organ purchased from Kirkstall Church, near Leeds" (where, by 1850, a large new Forster & Andrews instrument had been installed). This organ would almost certainly have been in the west gallery.

A restoration of the church in 1876 could possibly suggest the date of the appearance of the present Brindley & Foster - a 2-manual organ, divided north and south of the sanctuary area, originally with mechanical action running in a tunnel under the floor. J.H. Adkins added a Viol d'Orchestre to the Swell in 1932 and converted the whole action to pneumatic. Then in 1960 Messrs Henry Willis electrified it, leaving the stop-list as follows:

Divided organ by Brindley & Foster in Christ Church, Belper

GREAT		SWELL	
Open Diapason	8	Violin Diapason	8
Dulciana	8	Stop Diapason	8
Lieblich Gedact	8	Viol d'Orchestre	8
Principal	4	Vox Celeste	8
Lieblich Flute	4	Principal	4
Twelfth	2-2/3	Mixture (2 ranks)	
Fifteenth	2	Oboe	8

PEDAL	
Bourdon	16
Flute Bass	8

COUPLERS: unison, sub and octave
COMPASS: Manuals 61; Pedal 30
ACTION: electro-pneumatic

In 1986 it was overhauled by M.C. Thompson of Burton-on-Trent. The Adkins Viol was replaced by a Flageolet 2 while the Vox Celeste was returned to its original non-undulating form of a Vox Angelica. The Pedal Organ received a Choral Flute 4 – an extension of the existing unit rank.

Though some thirty feet apart, the two sides of the organ coalesce remarkably well and the acoustical ambiance of the building manages to create the impression of a much larger instrument.

CHURCH OF ST MARK, OPENWOODGATE
(Parish of St Peter, Belper)

Formerly a hamlet at the crossroads on the ridge to the east of Belper, Openwoodgate is now a spreading suburb within the main town boundary. As with Ambergate, the name is related to the fact that it was one of the entrances to the mediaeval forest of Duffield Frith.

A plain, aisleless Gothic building of 1891, St Mark's is not consecrated and remains a Mission Church within the town parish of St Peter's. Its pipe organ was presented by G.H. Strutt in 1905 and was placed in a tiny west gallery, very close to the ceiling.

Built by Stephen White of London, probably in 1796, it had stood in the Strutt family home at Bridge Hill House in Belper. The earliest reference to it is by Alexander Buckingham who, during the years 1822-4, added an octave of pedals, provided a bass to the Open Diapason and made a number of other mechanical alterations.

GREAT (GG)

Open Diapason	(8)
Stop Diapason	(8)
Dulciana (Fiddle-G)	(8)
Principal	(4)
Flute	(4)
Twelfth	(2-2/3)
Fifteenth	(2)
Sexquialtra (sic!) (3 & 2 ranks)	
Hautboy (Middle-C)	(8)

Later in the nineteenth century a small Swell Organ was added and the Great reduced to four stops (using part of the original chest). In this form, still with its attractive eighteenth century 3-tower case, it was installed in the gallery at St Mark's by J.H. Adkins. The same firm did some further work to the action in 1927. This included the provision of pneumatics to the Pedal as well as to some bass pipes of the Great Organ.

GREAT		SWELL	
Open Diapason Gt	(8)★	Violin Diapason	(8)
Stop Diapason Gt	(8)★	Gedact	(8)
Dolce	(8)	Principal Gt	(4)★
Flute Ch	(4)★	Hautboy	(8)★
		Tremulant	

PEDAL

Bourdon Ped	(16)

(containing 12 pipes from Buckingham's Diapason bass)

COUPLERS: 3 unison; Swell super octave
COMPASS: Manuals 56; Pedal 30
ACTION: Manuals mechanical; Pedal pneumatic
★ stops from 1796 organ

1796 Stephen White organ in St Mark's, Openwoodgate (until 1987)

With five stops surviving from the eighteenth century there was much that was charming about this organ, but, in its high, cramped position, it always suffered from temperature extremes. Eventually, in 1985, an electronic instrument was installed and, two years later, the old pipe organ was acquired by Martin Renshaw of Lyminge to be rebuilt as a house organ for Dr Francis Jackson, the distinguished Organist Emeritus of York Minster, by whom it is now much loved and cherished.

CHURCH OF ST SWITHUN, HOLBROOK ROAD
(Parish of St Peter, Belper)

St Swithun's Church was completed in 1913 and in that same year the first Organist was appointed – though there is no knowledge of the instrument that was used. The present organ was installed by Nelson & Co of Durham and was dedicated in 1951 as a War Memorial.

GREAT		SWELL	
Open Diapason	8	Lieblich Gedact	8
Dulciana	8	Viol d'Orchestre	8
Flute	8	Gemshorn	4
Geigen Principal	4	Oboe	8
		Tremulant	
PEDAL			
Bourdon	16		

COUPLERS: unison, sub and octave
COMPASS: Manuals 56; Pedal 30
ACTION: pneumatic

ANGLICAN CONVENT OF ST LAURENCE

The convent chapel was built in 1889, and this is the probable date of the organ by Lloyd of Nottingham which stood at the west end for nearly a hundred years.

GREAT		SWELL	
Open Diapason	8	Gamba	8
Dulciana	8	Vox Celeste	8
Lieblich Gedacht	8	Harmonic Flute	4
Principal	4		
Clarionet	8		
PEDAL			
Bourdon	16		

COUPLERS: 3 unison; Swell sub octave; Swell to
    Great super octave
COMPASS: Manuals 61; Pedal 30
ACTION: Manuals mechanical; Pedal pneumatic

In the late 1980's this organ was removed and replaced by a Casson "Positive". This, however, did not prove satisfactory and is itself, at the time of writing, in process of being superseded by an 1860 Bevington "Chancel Organ" (from a convent in Hammersmith) which is currently being installed by Mr David Roome of Belper.

BAPTIST CHURCH, BRIDGE STREET

An earlier chapel, built in 1818, still stands behind the shops opposite the present building of 1893. The latter is in Gothic style with a projecting "chancel" containing the baptistry.

The small 3-manual organ was originally in the house of T.B. Mellor, Organist of St Peter's, and was built in 1874 by J.M. Grunwell of Derby. The date of installation in the new Baptist chapel is not clear: tradition has it that it was 1901, though there is mention of an organ in Bulmer's 1895 Directory.

GREAT		SWELL	
Open Diapason	8	Gamba	8
Stopt Diapason	8	Gedact	8
Principal	4	Gemshorn	4
Fifteenth	2		
CHOIR		PEDAL	
Lieblich Gedact	8	Sub Bass	16
Dulciana	8	Gamba	8
Flute	4		
Clarionet	8		

COUPLERS: 5 unison
COMPASS: Manuals 58; Pedal 30
ACTION: mechanical

Grunwell's label tells us that he was "From Hill & Son, London". The pipework, certainly, is not inconsistent with such a claim and implication of quality.

In 1987, on account of the division of the building into upper and lower floors and the purchase of an electronic instrument, the Grunwell became surplus to requirements. It was dismantled by E.R. Stow of Derby and stored, later to be re-erected in St Peter's (qv) for use as a temporary organ, 1991-2. After a further period of substitution at the Queen's Hall Methodist Mission in Derby it arrived, in 1994, at its final resting place in Milford Parish Church (qv).

CONGREGATIONAL CHURCH, GREEN LANE

In the earlier part of the nineteenth century an organ was known to have been constructed by Joseph Gratian of Belper in the former 1790 chapel. The fine new Gothic chapel with its prominent spire was built in 1872. According to Bulmer's 1895 Directory there was "a large and sweet toned organ" with the inscription: "Presented to the Congregational Church by Ebenezer Smedley, Esq., May 26, 1886". It was built by C. Lloyd & Co of Nottingham and the cost was £350, "over and above £50 allowed for the old organ". In the 1920's it was rebuilt and enlarged by J.H. Adkins, when it probably acquired its pneumatic action. Following closure of the building in 1981 various of the pipes were used by other builders.

GREAT		SWELL	
Open Diapason	8	Lieblich Bourdon	16
Lieblich Gedact	8	Violin Diapason	8
Clarabella	8	Stopd Diapason	8
Dulciana	8	Viol d'Orchestre	8
Viol di Gamba	8	Voix Celeste	8
Principal	4	Gemshorn	4
Flauto Traverso	4	Lieblich Flute	4
Piccolo Harmonic	2	Fifteenth	2
Clarionet	8	Mixture (2 ranks)	
		Cornopean	8
PEDAL		Oboe Orchestra	8
Grand Open Diapason	16	Tremulant	
Grand Bourdon	16		

COUPLERS: unison, sub and octave
COMPASS: Manuals 61; Pedal 30
ACTION: pneumatic

CENTRAL METHODIST CHURCH, CHAPEL STREET
(former Wesleyan)

The first chapel was built in 1780 and soon acquired a reputation for its music. A Festival, advertised in 1804, contained a programme selected from the oratorios of Handel – "The Band will be numerous and the Chorusses (sic!) as full as possible", ran the announcement in the "Derby Mercury".

The present building dates from 1807 and may perhaps be described as a sort of Palladian Palace of the People. With an elegantly pedimented front and a fully galleried interior, accommodating (so it was said) 1,400 people, it was described as "the wonder of the country for many miles around"! Its singing continued to be celebrated and was led by "an efficient Band". Oratorios were frequently performed on Sunday afternoons.

In 1844 an organ chamber was built to the rear of the pulpit and the first organ erected under the direction of Thomas Mawkes – professional concert violinist, pupil of the composer, Spohr, and first Organist at the new St Peter's Church in Belper. The instrument had one manual of the "movable" type (– one which could slide into the case when not in use) and was probably installed by Joseph Gratian (who was certainly known to be tuning it by the early 1850's).

In 1873 the chapel was modernised and the organ sold for £35 to Kilburn Wesleyan in order to make room for a new 2-manual by Faulkner Bros of Manchester. Unfortunately this proved inadequate and in 1896 was replaced by the present instrument – a 2-manual by Cousans, Sons & Co of Lincoln, whose probable original specification (reconstructed from Scotchbrook's notes) was:

GREAT		SWELL	
Open Diapason	8	Lieblich Bourdon	16
Clarabella	8	Spitz Flute	8
Dulciana	8	Lieblich Gedackt	8
Principal	4	Viol de Gamba	8
Harmonic Flute	4	Celeste	8
Twelfth	2-2/3	Gemshorn	4
Fifteenth	2	Mixture (3 ranks)	
Clarinet	8	Cornopean	8
		Oboe	8
PEDAL		Tremulant	
Open Diapason	16		
Bourdon	16		
Bass Flute	8		

COUPLERS: 3 unison
ACTION: Manuals mechanical; Pedal pneumatic

J.H. Adkins enlarged it in 1913, when a Large Open Diapason and a Gamba were added to the Great, both on pneumatic action. In 1930 the same firm added Harmonic Bass 32 and Octave Diapason 8 to the Pedal; they also altered the Swell Spitz Flute and Viol de Gamba to Violin Diapason and Viol d'Orchestre respectively. Finally, in 1948, Messrs Nelson of Durham converted the whole manual action to pneumatic and provided super and suboctave couplers.

FIELD HEAD METHODIST CHURCH (former Primitive)

This chapel was built in 1822. The organ, by Hardy & Son of Stockport, bears the date 1910 on its soundboard. After demolition of the chapel in 1966 this organ was transferred (unchanged) to Zion Methodist Church, Openwoodgate (Belper) (qv).

GREAT		SWELL	
Open Diapason	8	Violin Diapason	8
Clarabella	8	Salicional	8
Dulciana	8	Gedackt	8
Wald Flute	4	Gemshorn	4
		Oboe	8
PEDAL		Tremulant	
Bourdon	16		

COUPLERS: 3 unison; Swell "Octaves"
COMPASS: Manuals 58; Pedal 30
ACTION: Manuals mechanical; Pedal pneumatic

HOLBROOK ROAD METHODIST CHURCH (former Primitive)

The chapel (closed in the 1980's) is of mid-nineteenth century type. Organists are listed from 1904 but no information is to hand about the organ.

POTTERY METHODIST CHURCH (former Wesleyan)

The chapel dates from 1816 and, in its early days, had a famous "Singing Pew" filled with "an efficient Choir and Band". It appears that "an organ was introduced" at some date before 1870. It was rebuilt in 1926 by J.H. Adkins and lasted until closure of the chapel in 1991.

GREAT		SWELL	
Open Diapason	8	Lieblich Gedact	8
Clarabella	8	Gamba	8
Dulciana	8	Vox Celeste	8
Principal	4	Gemshorn	4
Harmonic Flute	4	Oboe	8
		Tremulant	
PEDAL			
Bourdon	16		
(blank slider)			

COUPLERS: 3 unison; 1 prepared
COMPASS: Manuals: 56; Pedal 30
ACTION: Manuals mechanical; Pedal pneumatic

SALEM METHODIST CHURCH, GREEN LANE (former UMFC)

The chapel was built in 1856 and in 1871 Messrs Hill & Son are recorded as having put in an estimate for an organ – unsuccessfully, as it turned out. Who eventually got the contract we do not know, though the specification suggests an instrument of that period. From 1904 the organ was maintained by J.H. Adkins. Closure and demolition took place in the 1960's.

GREAT		SWELL	
Open Diapason	8	Gedact	8
Stop Diapason	8	Gamba	8
Dulciana	8	Gemshorn	4
Principal	4	Oboe	8
Fifteenth	2		
PEDAL			
Bourdon	16		

COUPLERS: 3 unison
ACTION: mechanical

ZION METHODIST CHURCH, OPENWOODGATE
(former UMFC)

This organ, by Hardy & Son of Stockport (1910), was installed in 1967, having been transferred (unchanged) from Field Head Methodist in Belper (qv). In 1994 it was overhauled and tonally remodelled by E.R. Stow of Derby – proof of how a seemingly unpromising small tracker instrument can be totally transformed into a viable musical entity.

GREAT		SWELL	
Open Diapason	8	Clarabella	8
Gedackt	8	Salicional	8
Principal	4	Wald Flute	4
Fifteenth	2	Gemshorn	2
PEDAL		Oboe	8
Bourdon	16	Tremulant	

COUPLERS: 3 unison
COMPASS: Manuals 58; Pedal 30
ACTION: Manuals mechanical; Pedal pneumatic

UNITARIAN CHAPEL, FIELD ROW

Built by Jedediah Strutt in 1788, this is the oldest functioning place of worship in Belper. It is still furnished with the original box pews which rise in tiers above the vaulted catacomb (accessible only from outside) containing the Strutt family remains in a series of shelf-like compartments.

"An organ" was put in the chapel in 1890 and an Organist and Choirmaster was appointed at £5 a year. "A Violoncello and Double Bass Violin", which had previously been used to lead the singing, were put up for sale. The "organ" in question appears, in fact, to have been a harmonium, which was replaced in 1937 by a Hammond electronic similar to the one installed the following year in St Peter's. However, in view of the facts that the Unitarians were not averse to organs and also that the Strutts (who endowed the chapel) were known to have possessed at least three chamber organs, it seems quite reasonable to suggest that there could have been a small pipe organ in this building during the earlier years of its existence.

JUBILEE HALL (SPIRITUALIST), NEW ROAD

The Hall was built in the Jubilee Year of 1887 and its organ was installed in 1899 – a 2-manual by G. Benson of Manchester.

GREAT		SWELL	
Open Diapason	8	Violin Diapason	8
Dulciana	8	Salicional	8
Hohl Flute	8	Gemshorn	4
Wald Flute	4	Oboe	8
PEDAL		Tremulant	
Bourdon	16		

COUPLERS: 3 unison; Swell octave
ACTION: Manuals mechanical; Pedal pneumatic

PUBLIC HALL, KING STREET

An imposing red-brick edifice, scene of many musical concerts and festivals in its heyday, but latterly converted for use as a cinema and then as a bingo hall. It was built in 1882, and in that same year the large Brindley & Foster organ was installed.

Though not originally conforming to the title-criterion of an organ in a church or chapel, this fine instrument was subsequently to become one – albeit only for a few years. In 1928 it was transferred by J.H. Adkins to the Kedleston Street Primitive Methodist Church in Derby, where it served until closure in the 1960's. After that it was acquired for private use by Mr. J.N. Handley of Breadsall. Parts of it eventually ended up in a home-made organ at the Darwin Comprehensive School in Chaddesden (– and see Holbrook Parish Church for the ultimate home of the Swell Cornopean).

The following uncredited specification is probably not the original one. It also differs in some details from that published on the occasion of the organ's re-opening at Kedleston Street. What it probably represents is the final version as it was in Belper.

GREAT		SWELL	
Open Diapason	8	Bourdon	16
Stop Diapason Bass	8	Open Diapason	8
Clarabella	8	Lieblich Gedact	8
Keraulophon	8	Salicional	8
Principal	4	Viol d'Amour	8
Wald Flute	4	Gemshorn	4
Fifteenth	2	Harmonic Piccolo	2
Mixture (3 ranks)		Mixture (2 ranks)	
Trumpet	8	Cornopean	8
		Orchestral Oboe	8
		Tremulant	
CHOIR (enclosed)		PEDAL	
Hohl Flute	8	Harmonic Bass	32
Dulciana	8	Open Diapason	16
Gemshorn	4	Bourdon	16
Harmonic Flute	4	Octave Diapason	8
Clarinet	8	Bass Flute	8
Tremulant			

COUPLERS, COMPASS & ACTION: unspecified

16 HEAGE

Yet another former chapelry within the ancient parish of Duffield. It is perhaps a little "inland" from the Derwent Valley but, on account of its one-time association with Duffield and its present proximity to Belper, it must surely be included in this survey.

PARISH CHURCH OF ST LUKE

A curiously fascinating building, in which the small chapel, rebuilt in the seventeenth century, had a large, plain, aisleless nave constructed across its west end in 1826, thus giving the church its distinctive overall T-plan.

In 1853 St Luke's acquired "from a neighbouring Township an excellent instrument at a moderate price". This can only be referring to the Snetzler organ formerly in St John's Chapel and then in St Peter's Church in Belper (qv). However, what was still regarded as "excellent" in 1853 was by 1877 (according to the local press) "unfit for use". It was consequently replaced in that year by a new organ, built by W Hedgeland of London at a cost of £250. It was placed at the north end of the transverse nave, from where it still speaks with a good, clear sonority.

1877 Hedgeland organ in Heage Church

GREAT		SWELL	
Open Diapason	8	Open Diapason	8
Stopped Diapason (Bass)	8	Lieblich Gedact	8
Clarabella Treble	8	Principal	4
Gamba	8	Oboe	8
Principal	4		
Flute	4		
Fifteenth	2		

PEDAL	
Bourdon	16

COUPLERS: 3 unison; Swell super octave to Great
COMPASS: Manuals 56; Pedal 30
ACTION: mechanical

An overhaul in 1993 by Anthony Herrod of Skegby saw the Swell Oboe very successfully replaced by a Gemshorn 2. This work on the organ is coupled with a proposed re-ordering of the church interior which will effectively bring the main worship entirely into the nave – and thus nearer to the organ.

EBENEZER METHODIST CHURCH (former UMFC)

This attractive little 1840's red-brick chapel on the Belper road closed in 1985 and has now been converted into a dwelling. It formerly had a small, anonymous organ that once stood in a private house; it was installed by J.H. Adkins in 1925. Following closure the organ went to a church in Manchester.

GREAT		SWELL	
Open Diapason	8	Lieblich Bass	8
Stop Diapason Bass	8	Lieblich Gedact	8
Claribella (sic!) Flute	8	Gamba	8
Dulciana	8	Principal	4
		Oboe	8
PEDAL		Tremulant	
Grand Bourdon	16		

COUPLERS: 3 unison
ACTION: mechanical

PARKSIDE METHODIST CHURCH (former Primitive)

Scotchbrook, in the period between the wars, gives the following specification:

GREAT		PEDAL	
Open Diapason	(8)	Bourdon	(16)
Stop Bass	(8)		
Dulciana	(8)		
Principal	(4)		

COUPLERS, COMPASS & ACTION: unspecified

By the 1980's, however, when a new chapel came to be built on an adjacent site, a totally different organ had been in service for some time – a small instrument (probably of the turn of the century) by W.E. Richardson of Manchester.

GREAT		SWELL	
Open Diapason	8	Lieblich Gedact	8
Stop Diapason	8	Dulciana	8
Gamba	8	Voix Celeste	8
		Flute	4
PEDAL			
Bourdon	16		

COUPLERS: 3 unison
ACTION: mechanical

With the opening of the new chapel this pipe organ was sold to Henry Groves of Nottingham and an electronic was installed.

NETHER HEAGE METHODIST CHURCH (former Primitive)

A simple stone chapel of 1878 with plain lancet windows, well-equipped with a modern suite of rooms to the rear and having a magnificent rural view across the valley towards the recently restored Heage Windmill.

The chapel's first organ was a harmonium, but this was replaced in 1924 or 1925 by the present pipe instrument, whose original date seems probably to have been of the 1880's. No labels remain, though features of the casework and specification suggest that it could have been by J.M. Grunwell of Derby. A faint inscription on the console lid can just be made out which reads "Chellaston Rectory 1889". It is certainly not inconceivable that it could have been a house organ – though, if this were so, the tall front pipes (13 lowest of the Open Diapason) would probably have been added at the 1920's installation.

Though at present suffering from a shortage of wind, it is nevertheless an effective and musical little instrument that will continue to give good service for a long time to come, given suitable care and maintenance.

GREAT		PEDAL	
Open Diapason	(8)	Bourdon	(16)
Stop Diapason Bass	(8)		
Stop Diapason Treble	(8)		
Dulciana	(8)		
Principal	(4)		
Flute	(4)		
Fifteenth	(2)		

COUPLER: "Pedals to Great"
COMPASS: Manual 56; Pedal 30
ACTION: mechanical

All stops are enclosed in a swell except for Bourdon and lowest 13 notes of the Open Diapason.

17 AMBERGATE

Situated where the River Amber joins the Derwent and a one-time major crossing point of the latter, Ambergate was a "gate" (or entrance) to the mediaeval forest of Duffield Frith. Later it was to become an important rail junction and the site of an enormous complex of kilns (connected with the limestone quarries at nearby Crich).

PARISH CHURCH OF ST ANNE

This church was opened and dedicated in 1892, though not fully consecrated until 1897. The organ was built by Alexander Young & Sons in 1894 and includes a characteristic feature of the firm – an "extended" Bass Flute on mechanical action.

GREAT		SWELL	
Open Diapason	8	Violin Diapason	8
Stpd Diap Clarabella	8	Salicional	8
Dulciana	8	Gemshorn	4
Flute	4	Oboe	8
PEDAL			
Bourdon	16		
Bass Flute	8		

COUPLERS: 3 unison; Swell to Great octave
COMPASS: Manuals 56; Pedal 30
ACTION: mechanical (including Pedal "extension")

METHODIST CHURCH, DEVONSHIRE STREET

In 1949 this chapel acquired the organ from Chevin Road Methodist in Milford (qv), the installation being by Jardine & Co of Manchester. Its specification at Ambergate (though not necessarily at Milford) was:

GREAT		SWELL	
Open Diapason	8	Gedact	8
Clarabella	8	Gamba	8
Principal	4	Flute	4
PEDAL		(blank slider – possibly used at some time in the past)	
Bourdon	16		

COUPLERS: 3 unison; Swell octave to Great
ACTION: mechanical

In the late 1980's the organ was totally rebuilt by M.C. Thompson of Burton-on-Trent with electric action and two unit extension ranks giving the following stops:

GREAT		SWELL	
Tenoroon	16	Diapason	8
Diapason	8	Rohr Flute	8
Rohr Flute	8	Flute	4
Principal	4	Flautino	2
Fifteenth	2		

PEDAL
Bourdon   16
Flute   8

    Tremulant (to all stops)
    COUPLERS: Great to Pedal; Swell to Pedal
    COMPASS: Manuals 61; Pedal 32
    ACTION: electric

The two extended ranks are: Bourdon/Flute 16 and Diapason 8.
In 1993 the instrument was disposed of in favour of an electronic one.

18 ALDERWASLEY

An ancient chapelry of Wirksworth parish, situated adjacent to Shining Cliff Woods, now a National Trust beauty spot on the west bank of the Derwent. The village has grown little since Francis Hurt in the 1780's established his forge down by the river, out of sight of his home at Alderwasley Hall.

CHAPEL OF ST MARGARET

Dating from the fifteenth century, this little building has been restored from dereliction and now serves as the village hall.

In 1828 Alexander Buckingham supplied a 3-stop barrel organ to "Francis Hurt Esqr at Alderwasley". It had one barrel containing ten hymn tunes. Fifteen years later he supplied a second barrel. As is so often the case in respect of these generous patrons, it is not clear whether the little organ was for use in the chapel or in the home.

Open Diapason to G	18 pipes
Stop Diapason	28 pipes
Principal	28 pipes

CHURCH OF ALL SAINTS

The new church was built by Mr Hurt in 1850 in the grounds of his mansion and the old chapel in the village consequently went out of use. The barrel organ may possibly have served in both buildings.

In 1880 a new organ was presented by Mr. A.F. Hurt and placed in the north transept. It was by Brindley & Foster of Sheffield and cost £477, plus a further £92 to lay on a water supply for the hydraulic blowing apparatus. It was clearly not a cheap organ: like the building, it was quite lavish, both tonally and visually.

After more than a century, with no alteration other than the provision of an electric blower and a balanced swell pedal, it is still a splendid instrument, typical of its builders at a period when they continued to reflect the tonal qualities of the great German builder, Edmund Schulze, with whom they had been closely associated. In 1990 it was given a sympathetic overhaul by J.H. Poyser of Derby.

GREAT		SWELL	
Open Diapason	8	Bourdon	16
Dulciana	8	Violin Diapason	8
Lieblich Gedact	8	Vox Angelica	8
Principal	4	Voix Celeste	8
Flauto Traverso	4	Salicet	4
Grave Mixture (2 ranks)		Full Mixture (3 ranks)	
Clarionet	8	Trumpet	8
		Oboe	8
PEDAL			
Subbass	16		
Violoncello	8		

COUPLERS: 3 unison; Great sub octave
COMPASS: Manuals 56; Pedal 29
ACTION: mechanical

1880 Brindley & Foster organ in Alderwasley Church

19   CRICH

The village, east of the Derwent, straggles up the side of an eminence known as Crich Stand which eventually rises to a height of nearly 1,000 feet. The church is at the top end of the village and is of substantial Norman origin, though it is the fourteenth century tower and spire that form its most prominent feature.

WAKEBRIDGE MANOR CHANTRY CHAPEL

Sir William de Wakeburge was a generous and pious patron of the parish during the fourteenth century and he was responsible for the construction of the new chancel and tower at the church. Additionally, in his own home (the site of which is now occupied by Wakebridge Farm) he built a chapel (or oratory) and furnished it with "an orgayne and other costly devises".

This is undoubtedly the earliest evidence of any organ in Derbyshire, pre-dating the Derby All Saints references by a century. In such a domestic oratory an organ would probably have been only of the "portative" (ie hand-held) type as frequently depicted in late mediaeval representations of angel musicians: an instrument with no more than a dozen or so pipes up to about a foot in length, in which one hand would operate a small bellows while the other would play a single-line melody on the minute keyboard.

1914 Hill organ in Crich Church

PARISH CHURCH OF ST MARY

There must have been an organ before 1914 since we find records of tuning visits by J.H. Adkins during the years 1903-7. It was in 1914 that W. Hill & Son of London built the small 3-manual pipe organ which, though now decommissioned, still remains in its loft at the west end of the nave. At that date it must have been one of the last instruments by the Hill firm before its amalgamation with Norman & Beard. It was a nice organ in its time, with some delicate Romantic tone-colours, though (typically of its period) lacking in upper chorus-work. The pneumatic action, however, gradually deteriorated to the point of unplayability and an electronic organ is now in regular use for worship.

GREAT		SWELL	
Double Dulciana	16	Geigen Principal	8
Open Diapason	8	Rohr Flute	8
Hohl Flute	8	Echo Gamba	8
Principal	4	Voix Celestes	8
Harmonic Flute	4	Gemshorn	4
Flautina	2	Oboe	8
		Tremulant	
CHOIR (enclosed)		PEDAL	
Lieblich Gedeckt	8	Bourdon	16
Dulciana	8	Bass Flute	8
Suabe Flute	4		
Clarinet	8		

COUPLERS: unison, sub and octave
COMPASS: Manuals 61; Pedal 30
ACTION: pneumatic
Detached console on floor at west end

BAPTIST CHURCH

The chapel dates (in its present form) from 1876 and stands imposingly, overlooking the market place at the centre of the village.

The organ is of considerable antiquity, internal evidence suggesting that it may have originated as a GG-compass instrument of the early nineteenth century. The fact that it was not new when acquired for the Baptist Church is borne out by the wording of the label: "From J.M. Grunwell . . ." (– who functioned in Derby during the last three decades of the nineteenth century). In all probability it started as a 1-manual and was then rebuilt by Grunwell when installed in the new chapel in 1876. Later, in 1904, J.H. Adkins added a Dulciana stop.

GREAT		SWELL	
Open Diapason	(8)	Stop Diapason	8
Stop Diapason	(8)	Dulciana	8
Principal	(4)	Principal	(4)
Fifteenth	(2)	Oboe	(8)

PEDAL
Bourdon (13 pipes)   16

    COUPLERS: 2 unison
    COMPASS: Manuals 56; Pedal 29
    ACTION: mechanical
    Casework with semicircular centre-pediment

The organ still functions and (at the time of writing) is still "in situ", though, since the donation of an electronic organ in 1990, this interesting old instrument has not been used and has been available for purchase.

1876 Grunwell organ in Crich Baptist Church (rebuilt from an older instrument)
(Drawing by Peter Greenwood)

FRITCHLEY CONGREGATIONAL CHURCH

Though within the parish of Crich, Fritchley is, in effect, a small village in its own right. Overlooking an extensive green is the attractive and architecturally stylish Congregational chapel, built in 1841. Tall, round-topped windows would suggest the existence of a gallery. There is no such gallery, however: the interior is high and open, with a flat, plastered ceiling – all factors conducive to making it a good musical auditorium.

The organ has seen a number of changes – notably a rebuild in 1947, in which a set of Oboe pipes was added (together with an electric blower). Various features of compass and tone quality would suggest a possible 1860's/70's date of origin. It is a pleasingly musical little instrument and one that is well-deserving of the overhaul that it now badly needs.

GREAT		PEDAL	
Small Open Diapason	8	Bourdon (20 pipes)	16
Stop Diapason	8		
Dulciana	8		
Principal	4		
Metallic Flute	4		
Oboe	8		
Tremulant			

COUPLER: Great to Pedal
COMPASS: Manual 54; Pedal 25
ACTION: mechanical
Enclosed in a swell except for Open Diapason and Bourdon

CRICH CARR METHODIST CHURCH (former Primitive)

This chapel, built in 1877, had a small pipe organ of later nineteenth century type. Following closure of the chapel in 1989 the organ was transferred to Tenbury Wells Methodist Church by John Davis of Cleobury Mortimer. From 1960 it had been maintained by the Johnson Organ Co of Derby and, at the time of closure, its specification and its pipework showed that some changes had taken place over the years.

GREAT		PEDAL	
Open Diapason	8	Bourdon (12 pipes)	16
Stopped Diapason Bass	8		
Stopped Diapason Treble	8		
Dulciana	8		
Flute	4		
Fifteenth	2		

COUPLER: Great to Pedal
ACTION: Manual mechanical; Pedal pneumatic
Enclosed in a swell except for Stopped Bass and Bourdon

20   DETHICK and HOLLOWAY

The two places are combined because Holloway, although now the major settlement with its own church, is still only a chapelry within the parish of Dethick (– itself now no more than a manorial cluster of farms around the mediaeval church). Together with Lea and Lea Bridge, the group of villages occupies a commanding position overlooking the intersection of the Lea Brook valley with the Derwent.

PARISH CHURCH OF ST JOHN THE BAPTIST, DETHICK

This small thirteenth century church with its magnificent early sixteenth century tower (provided by Anthony Babington of "Plot" fame), possessed only a reed organ until 1989, when a small, pedal-less instrument, built (probably in the early 1900's) by the Casson "Positive" Organ Co, was installed (following restoration) by M.C. Thompson of Burton-on-Trent.

GREAT
Double Bass (20 pipes)	16
Salicional	8
Open Diapason	8

    COUPLER: octave
    COMPASS: Bass-F, 49 notes
    ACTION: mechanical and pneumatic

Early C20th Casson "Positive" organ in Dethick Church

CHRIST CHURCH, HOLLOWAY

The impressive new church by P.H. Currey (1903), on a splendid hillside site, was furnished with a substantial organ by William Andrews of Bradford. Pipework is in a chamber to the north of the chancel and the detached console is on the opposite side.

GREAT		SWELL	
Bourdon	16	Geigen Principal	8
Open Diapason	8	Rohr Flöte	8
Viola	8	Echo Gamba	8
Claribel Flute	8	Voix Celeste	8
Salicional	8	Octave	4
Principal	4	Harmonic Flute	4
Wald Flute	4	Flautina	2
Grave Mixture (2 ranks)		Oboe	8
PEDAL		Tremulant	
Open Diapason	16		
Bourdon	16		
Flute	8		

COUPLERS: unison, sub and octave
COMPASS: Manuals 58; Pedal 30
ACTION: pneumatic

In this somewhat Germanic Romantic scheme it is interesting to note that every manual stop (except the Great Bourdon) was of full compass – a feature that was to prove useful in the 1988 rebuild, where many stops were able to be exchanged or transposed in order to give the organ a brighter and less foundational tone. In this same operation the pneumatic action was electrified and two stops were added to the Pedal. The builder responsible for this very successful transformation was M.C. Thompson of Burton-on-Trent.

GREAT		SWELL	
Double Diapason	16	Hohl Flute	8
Open Diapason	8	Salicional	8
Geigen Diapason	8	Voix Celeste	8
Lieblich Gedeckt	8	Gemshorn	4
Dulciana	8	Flute Harmonic	4
Principal	4	Piccolo	2
Wald Flute	4	Larigot	1-1/3
Twelfth	2-2/3	Oboe	8
Fifteenth	2	Tremulant	
PEDAL			
Open Diapason	16		
Sub Bass	16		
Bass Flute	8		
Open Diapason (Great)	8		
Super Octave (ex above)	4		

COUPLERS: unison and octave
COMPASS: Manuals 58; Pedal 30
ACTION: electro-pneumatic

HOLLOWAY METHODIST CHURCH (former UMFC)

The chapel is in lancet-Gothic style and occupies a dramatic hillside site. It originated in 1852 as one of a number of Wesleyan Reform chapels built by John Smedley, the local textile manufacturer and owner of the Hydro at Matlock. His characteristic liturgical aspirations resulted in slightly more "churchy" structures, often with towers, bells and chancels (– not to mention their own specially devised Prayer Book!).

In 1864 Holloway chapel became part of the UMFC and in 1879 it was doubled in size. What had been the original nave had a similar-sized aisle built alongside and the whole interior was then re-orientated through 90 degrees, the former chancel being partitioned off as a schoolroom.

The organ, by C. Lloyd "& Compy" of Nottingham, clearly dates from the building extension. It is pleasingly adequate though, at the time of writing, in need of a good clean and overhaul.

GREAT		PEDAL	
Open Diapason	8	Bourdon (20 pipes)	16
Gemshorn	4		
Dulciana	8★		
Stopd Diapason	8★		
Lieblich Flute	4★		
Oboe	8★		
Tremulant (a later addition)			

COUPLER: Pedal coupler
COMPASS: Manual 56; Pedal 30
ACTION: mechanical
★ stops enclosed in a swell

21 CROMFORD

The history of St Mary's Church, of Willersley Castle, of the various mills and, indeed, of the whole village of Cromford is linked inextricably to one outstanding figure: Sir Richard Arkwright. It was his vision that recognized the potential of the site and it was his dynamic drive that caused Cromford eventually to become a shrine, revered as a cradle of the Industrial Revolution.

WILLERSLEY CASTLE

Commenced in 1789 as the intended residence of Sir Richard, the castle is a Romantic "Gothic" pile, strategically hidden from the seething mill complex. The diarist, John Byng, visited the site in 1790 while the castle was under construction and had this to say: "There is like wise a music room; this is upstairs, is 18 feet square, and will have a large organ in it". Unfortunately this was not to be, since, when nearing completion the following year, the whole place was badly damaged by fire. Arkwright himself died in 1792 and consequently never took up residence in the Castle.

There is no record of any organ in inventories of furnishings subsequent to the fire. The house is now a Methodist Guild Holiday and Conference Centre.

PARISH CHURCH OF ST MARY

This was commenced by Sir Richard Arkwright as a chapel for the Castle but was only completed and consecrated in 1797, five years after the death of its founder.

First mention of any organ in the church is by Archdeacon Butler on his 1824 Visitation, but no details are given other than that it was "in gallery".

It is Alexander Buckingham in 1828 who supplies us with fuller information:

> "Richard Arkwright Esqr. at Willersley Castle near Matlock
> – An organ with one set of keys from GG long octaves to E
> in alt with a piano movement to take off the chorus stops".

Open Diapason to gamut G in front	46 pipes	(8)
Stop Diapason	57 pipes	(8)
Principal	57 pipes	(4)
Fifteenth	57 pipes	(2)
Sexqualtra bafs 4 ranks	112 pipes	
Cornet treble 4 ranks	116 pipes	
Trumpet bafs and treble	57 pipes	(8)
	502 pipes	

> "The bellows are diagonal. The Trumpet is in a very bad state not used. The organ has been very ill-used the Sexqualtra and Cornet pipes have been mix'd and changed from their original state. In a mahogany case 12ft. high, 6ft. 1½in. wide, 3ft. deep. Willersley Castle 28 July, 1828. A.B."

A further note three months later reads:

> "There is a barrel added since it was in this Chapel but it cannot now be used. There is a date on the keys of May 17, 1770 but the organ was brought here from Staunton Harold the seat of Earl Ferrers and purchased by Sir Richard Arkwright, it now stands in Cromford Chapel and repaired by A Buckingham, October 1828."

The Staunton Harold reference is very interesting and clearly needs further investigation, especially in view of the continued existence of an even earlier historic organ in the church at that place. Was the instrument described above in the house (rather than the church) at Staunton Harold? And was this organ, purchased by the original Sir Richard, the "large organ" once destined for the music room in Willersley Castle?

White's 1857 Directory mentions that in the church there was "an organ, which was put up several years ago, to which many additions and improvements have since been made". This old organ was not to last much longer, though, for in 1858 a total refurbishment of the church in Gothic style was carried out by the Derby architect, H I Stevens, and in the following year a new organ was ordered from W. Hill & Son of London:

"Mr Arkwright, Cromford   Feb 10 (1859)   Estimate for new Org 2 manuals"

GREAT		SWELL (Tenor-C)	
Open Diapason	(8)	Open Diapason	(8)
Stop Diapason	(8)	Stop Diapason	(8)
Principal	(4)	Cornopean	(8)
Flute	(4)		
Twelfth	(2-2/3)		
Fifteenth	(2)		

PEDAL
Bourdon (1 octave)   (16)

COUPLERS: 2 unison
ACTION: mechanical

Complete with "2 comps, oak case, gilt front pipes", it cost £240 "ex carriage", but a note then follows in the Hill Letter Book that it was "ordered without Swell" (– order No 1019). The "Wirksworth Advertiser" of 21 May 1859 describes the organ as having eight stops (– obviously the six Great ones plus Bourdon and Pedal coupler) and there is nothing further to suggest that the proposed Hill Swell was ever added.

The present 2-manual format dates from the 1870's when Lloyd of Nottingham "Enlarged & improved" it. Minor modifications have since occured, notably a 30-note pedalboard fitted by Willis in 1959. A water leak from the tower in 1991 rendered the Swell and Pedal unplayable. Restoration plans have been considered but have had to be shelved in favour of priority work to the building itself.

GREAT		SWELL (Tenor-C:	
Open Diapason	8	Bass coupled to Great)	
Stop Diapason Bass	8	Open Diapason	8
Stop Diapason	8	Viol d'Orchestre	8
Dulciana	8	Keraulophon	8
Flute	4	Principal	4
Principal	4	Oboe	8
Fifteenth	2	Tremulant	
Clarabella	8		

PEDAL
Grand Bourdon   16 (originally 20 pipes)

COUPLERS: "Swell to Great Manual"; "Pedal Coupler"
COMPASS: Manuals 54; Pedal 30
ACTION: mechanical (top 10 Bourdons pneumatic)
Drawstops in horizontal row over Swell keys

Hill/Lloyd organ in Cromford Church

LADY GLENORCHY'S CHAPEL (Congregational)

Situated on the A6, just south of Arkwright's red-brick Masson Mill, this former Independent chapel was opened in 1785 and demolished in 1951 when the road was widened. An organ was installed – probably at the end of the nineteenth century – by Albert Keates of Sheffield. After closure it was transferred to Alvaston Congregational (now URC) in Derby where it had the following stop-list:

GREAT		SWELL	
Open Diapason	8	Violin Diapason	8
Dulciana	8	Stopped Diapason	8
Rohr Flute	8	Viol di Gamba	8
Principal	4	Flute	4
		Fifteenth	2
PEDAL		Oboe	8
Bourdon	16	Tremulant	
Bass Flute	8		

COUPLERS: 3 unison
COMPASS: Manuals 56; Pedal 30
ACTION: Manuals mechanical; Pedal pneumatic

Early in 1995, in preparation for alterations to the interior of the Alvaston chapel, this instrument was disposed of in favour of an electronic one.

METHODIST CHURCH (former Wesleyan)

The chapel is a spacious, apsed building of late nineteenth century type, with a suite of schoolrooms attached. It is in Water Lane, facing across the Greyhound Pool.

The organ – of generous sonority – came from the now closed Mount Tabor UMFC chapel on the opposite side of the Pool, where it had been rebuilt by J.H. Adkins in 1912. The low format, with rounded corners of 8ft pipes going right down to floor level, indicates a previous location of restricted height, such as in a gallery, close to the ceiling.

The Fifteenth must be a recent alteration – perhaps transposed from a former Principal 4.

GREAT		SWELL	
Open Diapason	8	Open Diapason	8
Rohr Gedacht	8	Salicional	8
Dulciana	8	Gemshorn	4
Wald Flute	4		
Fifteenth	2		

PEDAL
Double Diapason   16 (top 6 pipes open metal)

COUPLERS: 3 unison
COMPASS: Manuals 61; Pedal 30
ACTION: pneumatic

22 BONSALL

Bonsall is a small hill-village on the high ground west of the Heights of Abraham. With a large church of thirteenth century origin, an ancient market cross and a number of good seventeenth and eighteenth century houses, it was clearly once a more important place (– a centre for framework knitting) than its present remoteness would suggest.

PARISH CHURCH OF ST JAMES

The church formerly possessed an organ by Jardine of Manchester, about which no details are now remembered except that it had a Tenor-C Swell. It could possibly have dated from the 1863 rebuilding of the church.

The present organ was installed in the 1960's by H. Groves of Nottingham. It is a 1926 pneumatic instrument by C. Lloyd & Co and stands at the west end of the south aisle.

GREAT		SWELL	
Open Diapason	8	Violin Diapason	8
Hohl Flute	8	Lieblich Gedact	8
Dulciana	8	Salicional	8
Principal	4	Gemshorn	4
Fifteenth	2	Cornopean	8
PEDAL		Tremulant	
Bourdon	16		

COUPLERS: unison, sub and octave
COMPASS: Manuals 61; Pedal 32
ACTION: pneumatic (including stop-keys)

23   MATLOCK BATH

Matlock Bath is a spa town stretched along a strip of the west bank of the Derwent at a point where the valley is both narrow and steeply sided, giving it something of the appearance of the small towns in the Mosel valley and its tributaries. Unusually for Derbyshire the Georgian and Regency houses facing the promenade are stuccoed and painted in bright colours.

The Old Bath Hotel was a popular venue for concerts, even featuring (in 1760) a performance by Miss Patty Greatorex, daughter of the North Wingfield Organist, Anthony Greatorex (a well-known local musician whose son, Thomas, later became Organist of Westminster Abbey): she was reported as having played "several little pieces on the Organ" (presumably on a chamber organ set up for the occasion).

PARISH CHURCH OF HOLY TRINITY

This attractive cruciform Gothic church with its slender spire was built in 1842 and enlarged in 1873.

The first organ was put into a gallery in the tower in 1844 by Bevington & Sons of London. Following the extensions of 1873 it was moved into a new chamber on the "north" of the chancel. In this position it almost certainly proved to be totally inadequate.

A new organ was built in 1876 by W. Hill & Son. Subsequently a few alterations were made: a Tremulant was added in 1906 and in 1930 a Bass Flute (together with the associated Pedal pneumatic action). On the whole, though, the Hill organ remained virtually unaltered until it fell into disuse and neglect during the 1970's when, in 1975, it was succeeded by an electronic instrument. Finally, in 1993, it was removed from the church and some of the pipes were put into safe-keeping by members of the Arkwright Society from Cromford.

GREAT		SWELL	
Open Diapason	8	Open Diapason	8
Hohl Flute	8	Gedact	8
Dulciana	8	Salicional	8
Principal	4	Principal	4
Wald Flute	4	Flautina	2
Fifteenth	2	Oboe	8
(prepared slider for Mixture)		Tremulant	

PEDAL
Bourdon   16
Bass Flute   8

COUPLERS: 3 unison
COMPASS: Manuals 56; Pedal 30
ACTION: Manuals mechanical; Pedal pneumatic

METHODIST CHURCH (former Wesleyan)

Opened in 1865, this must be a very early example of a mainstream Wesleyan chapel boasting a tower and spire. Now used for commercial purposes, it occupies a prominent place in the main parade of buildings along the river front.

The specification of the organ is given by Scotchbrook and it would appear to be an instrument of the 1880's, maybe by Lloyd of Nottingham.

GREAT		PEDAL	
Open Diapason	8	Bourdon	16
Stop Bass	8		
Clarabella	8		
Dulciana	8		
Keraulophon	8		
Principal	4		
Fifteenth	2		
Oboe	8		
Tremulant			

COUPLER: Manual to Pedal
ACTION: mechanical

24 MATLOCK

North of Matlock Bath the valley develops into a narrow limestone gorge. To the west are the Heights of Abraham (now reached by cable-car) and on the east is High Tor, to the north of which is old Matlock. The churchyard of St Giles rises up to a high point which gives a good view of the valley below. From here one can also see northwards to Matlock Bank where the spa grew as the hydros proliferated during the later part of the nineteenth century.

PARISH CHURCH OF ST GILES

Little more than the fifteenth century tower remains of the mediaeval church: the chancel was rebuilt in 1859 and the nave in 1871.

The earliest organ (known to have existed before 1820) was by Flight & Robson and was probably a barrel organ. This was replaced in 1844 by "a small organ" in the west gallery costing about £100 (– an amount that would have represented a 1-manual instrument with half-a-dozen stops or more). This same small organ was described in 1870 as being "accompanied by fiddles, clarinet and bassoon".

The rebuilding of the nave was followed in 1873 by the installation of a substantial new organ by Brindley & Foster of Sheffield – a large 2-manual to which a Choir Organ and various other stops were added by J.H. Adkins in 1908. At the latter date it was furnished with magnificent twin case-fronts, carved by Mr Advent Hunstone of Tideswell, in a rich, late-Gothic style that matched the new stalls and screen. One case faced south across the chancel and was integral with the stalls; the other faced west into the vestry and, through the same, into the north aisle. A small engraved representation of the chancel case was to become the letter-heading "logo" for the firm of J.H. Adkins.

Advent Hunstone casework at St Giles', Matlock

83

GREAT		SWELL	
(blank slider)		Lieblich Bourdon	16
Diapason Phonon	8	Violin Diapason	8
Open Diapason	8	Rohr Flöte	8
Hohl Flöte	8	Gamba	8
Octave Diapason	4	Voix Celestes	8
Harmonic Flute	4	Vox Angelica	8
Twelfth	2-2/3	Salicet	4
Fifteenth	2	Flûte à Cheminée	4
Trumpet	8	Mixture (3 ranks)	
		Oboe	8
		Cornopean	8
		Tremulant	

CHOIR (enclosed)		PEDAL	
Lieblich Gedeckt	8	Harmonic Bass	32
Dulciana	8	Contra Bass	16
Wald Flute	4	Bourdon	16
Piccolo	2	Octave	8
Clarionet	8	Flute Bass	8
(blank slider)			

COUPLERS: unison, sub and octave
COMPASS: Manuals 61; Pedal 30
ACTION: pneumatic

By the late 1980's the organ had become very unreliable with (eventually) only the Great playable. Not only was it large and therefore expensive to maintain, but parts of it (especially the Pedal Organ) were deeply buried and virtually inaccessible. It has therefore been proposed that a smaller organ, using the best of the existing material, should be built in a new gallery at the west end. It will be fronted by the Hunstone case from the vestry.

PARISH CHURCH OF ALL SAINTS, MATLOCK BANK

This might indeed have been a wonderful church had it ever been completed. What we have is a lofty choir completed in 1884 to a design by T.H. and F. Healey, together with a part of a nave hastily finished in truncated form at a later date.

The organ was built by Forster & Andrews of Hull in 1886 and cost the not inconsiderable sum of "upwards of £500". It had an interesting Schulze-like specification which included no fewer than nine mixture ranks. Even so, it is difficult to believe that it would have suited the much larger building that was originally planned. As things have turned out, though, it is right for its surroundings and sounds very fine.

GREAT		SWELL	
Open Diapason	8	Lieblich Bordun	16
Dulciana	8	Violin Diapason	8
Rohrflöte	8	Gamba	8
Octave Diapason	4	Voix Celestes	8
Waldflöte	4	Octave Diapason	4
Mixture (4 ranks)		Dulciana Cornet (5 ranks)	
Clarinet	8	Trumpet	8
		Oboe & Bassoon	8
PEDAL		Tremulant	
Contra Bass	16		
Violoncello	8		
Flute Bass	8		

COUPLERS: 3 unison; Swell sub; Swell octave
COMPASS: Manuals 61; Pedal 30
ACTION: mechanical

In 1961 J W Walker of London divided the Dulciana Cornet into two separately drawing stops: Scharf (2 ranks: 19-22) and Mixture (3 ranks: 24-26-29). Then in 1982 the organ was overhauled by Midland Organ Builders and a 2ft Principal was added to the Great – a stop which is clearly of musical benefit. At the same time the Swell Scharf was replaced by a 2ft Fifteenth – again a useful stop, though one here regrets a little the break-up of an interesting and unusual mixture scheme.

CONGREGATIONAL CHURCH, FARLEY HILL

This pleasantly situated chapel dates from 1901. It consists of a nave and a "south" aisle, the latter now being partitioned off, except for the "east" end which is retained as an organ chamber.

The organ is fascinating. It was built by G. Benson of Manchester, probably in the 1880's or 90's, for a house in Great Longstone. In 1908 it was installed at Farley by J.H. Adkins. Its design is remarkable in that, on to a fairly conventional late Victorian instrument (of good quality) there is superimposed (– literally, for indeed it is constructed above the rest of the organ) a Solo Organ played from a third manual and whose tracker mechanism rises up immediately behind the show-pipes of the facade.

There were repairs by J.H. Adkins in 1927 and 1950 and one can only assume that eventually the Solo section became too difficult to maintain. In 1979 the Johnson Organ Co of Derby overhauled the basic two manuals, disconnecting (regrettably) the unique Solo Organ.

GREAT		SWELL	
Open Diapason	8	Open Diapason	8
Small Open Diapason	8	Keraulophon	8
Clarabella	8	Dulcet	4
Dulciana	8	Oboe	8
Principal	4		

SOLO		PEDAL	
Viol de Gamba	8	Open Diapason	16
Viol d'Amour	8	Bourdon	16
Harmonic Flute	4		
Orchestral Oboe	8		
Cornopean	8		
Clarionet	8		

COUPLERS: 3 unison; Solo to Great
COMPASS: Manuals 56; Pedal 30
ACTION: mechanical

Late C19th Benson organ in Farley Hill Congregational Church

METHODIST & UNITED REFORMED CHURCH, BANK ROAD

This substantial one-time Wesleyan chapel, built in 1882 and with a tower and spire added in 1904, is now the main centre of Free Church influence within Matlock town, having been joined by the local URC congregation following closure of their own church (qv).

The organ was built by Bevington & Sons of London and appears on that firm's c1885 list. It was renovated by J.H. Adkins in 1909 and Scotchbrook gives its specification as:

GREAT		SWELL	
Open Diapason	8	Violin Diapason	8
Hohl Flute	8	Rohr Flute	8
Dulciana	8	Vox Angelica	8
Principal	4	Vox Celeste	8
Harmonic Flute	4	Geigen Principal	4
Clarionet	8	Fifteenth	2
		Mixture	
PEDAL		Cor Anglais	8
Bourdon	16	Tremulant	
Bass Flute	8		

COUPLERS: 3 unison
COMPASS & ACTION: not given

In 1968 the organ was rebuilt with electro-pneumatic action by Henry Groves of Nottingham. Some improvements were made to the specification though, for a large building, it is still only a relatively small instrument, lacking especially in reed tone of the Trumpet variety.

GREAT		SWELL	
Open Diapason	8	Violin Diapason	8
Hohl Flöte	8	Rohr Flöte	8
Dulciana	8	Vox Angelica	8
Principal	4	Voix Celestes	8
Harmonic Flute	4	Geigen Principal	4
Fifteenth	2	Flageolet	2
		Mixture (2 ranks)	
PEDAL		Oboe	8
Bourdon	16	Tremulant	
Bass Flute	8		

COUPLERS: 3 unison; Swell super octave
COMPASS: Manuals 56; Pedal 30
ACTION: electro-pneumatic

METHODIST CHURCH, BANK ROAD (former Primitive)

A hundred yards or so from the former Wesleyan chapel stands this fine Gothic building which, with its adjacent schoolroom in the same style, dates from 1878. After closure it became the "Chapel Annexe" of the old Matlock College of Higher Education.

The organ was built by Brindley & Foster of Sheffield, probably in 1886; it was rebuilt by J.H. Adkins in 1904 and again (with pneumatic action) in 1926.

GREAT		SWELL	
Open Diapason	8	Lieblich Bourdon	16
Open Diapason	8	Open Diapason	8
Dulciana	8	Lieblich Gedact	8
Hohl Flute	8	Salcional	8
Octave Diapason	4	Vox Celeste	8
Harmonic Flute	4	Salicet	4
Fifteenth	2	Mixture (3 ranks)	
Tromba	8	Cornopean	8
		Oboe	8
		Tremulant	

CHOIR (probably enclosed)		PEDAL	
Violincelle (sic!)	8	Harmonic Bass	32
Clarabella Flute	8	Open Diapason	16
Dolce	8	Bourdon	16
Wald Flute	4	Octave Diapason	8
Lieblich Piccolo	2	Flute Bass	8
Clarionet	8		
Vox Humana	8		
Tromba	8		
Tremulant			

COUPLERS & COMPASS: not given by Scotchbrook
ACTION: pneumatic

The disappearance of this apparently fine organ from Matlock must have been a sad loss and one is tempted to wonder why it could not have been transferred to the surviving Methodist chapel just down the road.

METHODIST CHURCH, IMPERIAL ROAD (former UMFC)

Adkins' accounts give: "1911. To removing & re-erecting Organ in New Church . . . To adding to Swell Organ Oboe 8ft . . . To providing New Show Front in Arch & silvering all Front pipes". The stop-list in Scotchbrook's notebook shows us that it was a small 2-manual by Lloyd of Nottingham – a very limited instrument compared with those in Matlock's other town-centre churches. In fact, looked at on paper, the specification has the appearance of that of a 1-manual instrument, split up (perhaps by Adkins?) to cover two keyboards.

GREAT		SWELL	
Open Diapason	8	Stop Diapason	8
Clarabella	8	Gamba	8
Principal	4	Flute	4
		Oboe	8
PEDAL			
Bourdon	16		

COUPLERS: 3 unison
COMPASS & ACTION: not given

After closure the building was bought by Matlock Town Council and became known as the Imperial Rooms.

STARKHOLMES METHODIST CHURCH (former Primitive)

Built in 1905, this fairly standard small Edwardian Gothic chapel lasted less than ninety years, having been closed in 1993 and sold the following year for redevelopment. The writer's wish would be that he had discovered the organ here before such closure, while it was still playable. A temporary saving operation, however, has been put into effect and the instrument is now stored in the hope that a sympathetic home will be found for it in due course.

c1870 Grunwell rebuild in Starkholmes Methodist Church of c1840 organ

The organ was installed in 1905 by J.H. Adkins, who (unusually) seems to have made no alterations of his own. The attractive casework of battlemented Gothic is in 1840's style, though the specification suggests a rebuild of the 1870's – an observation that was confirmed when the instrument was dismantled in November 1994 by E.R. Stow of Derby.

A label behind the facia board revealed that (in its presumed 1870's version) it was "from J.M. Grunwell, Organ Builder, Derby". Furthermore, although virtually all existing pipework appears to date from the rebuild, it was discovered that the chest and parts of the mechanism were older and that the Open Diapason (positioned at the front) was located over the bored holes of a 2 to 3-ranks compound stop – which presumably would have been a Sesquialtera at the period in question. It was also concluded that the manual compass of 58 notes was a transposition of an old "long" one from GG (but without GG sharp – a common enough space-saving economy).

As far as one can judge from the conservative 1870's classical specification of six stops up to 2ft pitch with a small-scale Pedal stop to enhance the bass, it would seem to conform to the ideal of a small church organ. With the additional earlier elements (including the fine case) the historical importance of this little instrument is greatly increased and it becomes all the more vital that its period of storage should be only of minimal duration.

GREAT		PEDAL	
Open Diapason	8	Sub Bass	16
Lieblich Gedact	8		
Dulciana	8		
Principal	4		
Flute	4		
Fifteenth	2		

COUPLER: Keys to Pedals
COMPASS: Manuals 58; Pedal 25
ACTION: mechanical

RC CHURCH OF OUR LADY & ST JOSEPH

This must be the smallest organ in Derbyshire. It is what used to be referred to as a "plainsong organ", having but two stops (loud and soft) contained within a quite attractive chamber organ-like case and situated on the north side of the sanctuary. The probable date is around 1900 but, unlike the other mini-organs of that period (notably the Casson "Positive" instruments), its keyboard is of full compass.

GREAT	
Open Diapason	8
Dulciana	8

No pedals; no couplers
COMPASS: Manual 56

UNITED REFORMED CHURCH, CHESTERFIELD ROAD

The former Congregational Church is demolished and its members have merged with those of Matlock Methodist at the one-time Wesleyan Chapel (qv). The schoolroom survives and is now used by the Assemblies of God (Pentecostal).The church, dating from 1866, was a fine building in Early English Gothic style with a tall, slender spire. An old photograph of the interior shows a very Anglican-looking arrangement with the organ in a chamber to the north of the chancel. The instrument itself was built in 1878 by C. Lloyd & Co of Nottingham (– it may have been not unlike the same firm's 1886 instrument at Belper Congregational [qv]), enlarged by J.H. Adkins in 1907 and rebuilt by the same with pneumatic action in 1929. On this latter occasion the re-opening recital was by Reginald Goss-Custard of Liverpool Cathedral. Various other additions continued to be commissioned from Adkins by Major H. Douglas who, as well as being a pillar of the church, was Manager of the nearby Smedley's Hydro.

GREAT		SWELL	
Diapason Phonon	8	Lieblich Bourdon	16
Open Diapason	8	Open Diapason	8
Gamba	8	Stop Diapason	8
Hohl Flute	8	Dulciana	8
Dulciana	8	Voix Celeste	8
Principal	4	Flûte Harmonique	4
Wald Flute	4	Piccolo	2
Fifteenth	2	Mixture (3 ranks)	
Tromba	8	Contra Fagotto	16
Oboe	8	Cornopean	8
Clarinet	8	Oboe	8
Vox Humana	8	Clarinet	8
		Vox Humana	8
PEDAL			
Harmonic Bass	32		
Open Diapason	16		
Bourdon	16		
Dolce Bass	16		
Bass Flute	8		
Trombone	16		
Tromba	8		

COUPLERS: Unison, sub and octave; Great octave
ACTION: the duplexed reed stops suggest that Adkins'
   1929 pneumatics may have eventually been electrified

25 TANSLEY

From Matlock the A615 Wessington road runs eastwards alongside Matlock Cliff and very soon passes the small village of Tansley, situated on the edge of the Moor that bears its name.

PARISH CHURCH OF HOLY TRINITY

The small church dates from 1840 and is in the simplest Early English style of the period. A north aisle was added in 1870.

In 1850 a Flight & Robson barrel organ of six stops (with five barrels of ten tunes each) was bought from the church at South Elkington (Lincs) and installed in the west gallery by Forster & Andrews of Hull. Shortly afterwards it was converted to manual keyboard operation and later some pedals were added.

In 1896 a new 2-manual organ was constructed (still in the gallery) by John Stacey of Derby, the flue pipework of the old instrument being incorporated into the new Swell Organ (– it is still possible to see that the middle compass of the Swell pipes, equivalent to that of a small barrel instrument, consists of much older material).

Tansley Church, showing 1896 Stacey organ

Stacey himself seems to be something of a shadowy figure with only a couple of other known instruments, both in Derby itself. What induced him to come out to Tansley we do not know. Some correspondence in the church archives reveals him as having been a fairly simple soul:

> "All being well I hope to bring you the Organ on Thursday next,
> ie if we can have the Man and horses, I have just been after them
> but they are all off Hay-making, ... what about lodgings, I only
> want a clean place & the plainest of cooking"

A delightful insight into life a century ago, not to mention a charming disregard for punctuation!

GREAT		SWELL	
Open Diapason	8	Open Diapason	8
Clarabella	8	Stop Diapason Bass	8
Viol di Gamba	8	Gedact	8
Principal	4	Octave	4
Flute	4	Fifteenth	2
		Trumpet	8
PEDAL			
Pedal Bourdon	16		
Flute	8		

COUPLERS: 3 unison
COMPASS: Manuals 58; Pedal 30
ACTION: Manuals mechanical; Pedal pneumatic

A Tremulant was added to the Swell Organ in 1937 by Bertram Hopkinson of Ashover and, in 1989, the Johnson Organ Co of Derby overhauled the organ and added a Fifteenth to the Great in place of the Flute. With its newly-enhanced late-Victorian Great and its five Swell stops (-all except the Trumpet) which survive from the original early nineteenth century barrel organ, this is without doubt an instrument of interesting and historic character.

26 SOUTH DARLEY (also known as WENSLEY)

The small village of Wensley is situated on the road from Darley Dale that climbs up what is confusingly known as Wensleydale towards the old lead-mining town of Winster.

PARISH CHURCH OF ST MARY THE VIRGIN

This church serves the village of Wensley, although the location name of South Darley is more commonly adhered to. It is a small neo-Norman structure of the 1840's with a chancel of 1866.

The organ is on the south side of the chancel and was built in 1902 by Wadsworth & Bro of Manchester. It was then rebuilt and enlarged by J.H. Adkins in 1927.

GREAT		SWELL	
Open Diapason	8	Open Diapason	8
Stopt Diapason	8	Lieblich Gedact	8
Dulciana	8	Echo Gamba	8
Harmonic Flute	4	Voix Celestes	8
PEDAL		Gemshorn	4
Bourdon	16	Oboe	8
Bass Flute	8	Tremulant	

COUPLERS: 3 unison; Swell octave
COMPASS: Manuals 56; Pedal 30
ACTION: Manuals mechanical; Pedal pneumatic

Although uninspiring on paper, it is a good example of how effective such a limited instrument can be when placed in a favourable, open position and when the plastered wall surfaces of the church provide the right sort of acoustics. In 1989 it was overhauled by J.H. Poyser who added a very well-blending Fifteenth 2 in place of the rather unpleasant Swell Oboe.

1902 Wadsworth organ in South Darley Church

27 *DARLEY DALE*

North of Matlock the Dale, still dominated by the River Derwent, the A6 road and the former Midland Railway (now revived as Peak Rail), contains a succession of communities – most of them of industrial origin, though the nucleus of the mediaeval Darley village is still evident in the vicinity of the church.

PARISH CHURCH OF ST HELEN

A large and architecturally interesting church of thirteenth century origin. Its cruciform plan is not inappropriate to its latter-day "collegiate" function as the focal centre of a Local Ecumenical Project based on the two Anglican and three Methodist churches within the parish.

The organ started life as a 2-manual tracker instrument by Brindley & Foster of Sheffield, probably not unlike that of 1880 which still remains unaltered at Alderwasley (qv). In 1908 J.H. Adkins of Derby carried out a "renovation, addition and alteration" which included a new Tremulant and an extra rank for the Mixture stop. It is not clear, though, whether he did anything to the action at this stage.

GREAT		SWELL	
Open Diapason	8	Lieblich Bourdon	16
Dulciana	8	Violin Diapason	8
Rohr Flute	8	Lieblich Gedact	8
Octave Diapason	4	Viole d'Orchestre	8
Flute	4	Voix Celeste	8
Super Octave	2	Salicet	4
		Lieblich Piccolo	2
PEDAL		Mixture (3 ranks)	
Bourdon	16	Cornopean	8
Flute Bass	8	Oboe	8
		Tremulant	

COUPLERS: 3 unison; Swell octave
COMPASS: Manuals 56; Pedal 30
ACTION: possibly pneumatic from 1908

During the 1960's H. Groves of Nottingham converted the action to electro-pneumatic and some extra stops were added. Despite alterations the instrument still has a strong B&F character, though the new Great Mixture has an uncomfortable "break-back" in an exposed part of its compass.

GREAT		SWELL	
Open Diapason	8	Violin Diapason	8
Dulciana	8	Lieblich Gedact	8
Rohr Flöte	8	Viol d'Orchestre	8
Octave Diapason	4	Voix Celestes	8
Flute	4	Salicet	4
Super Octave	2	Nazard	2-2/3
Mixture (2 ranks)		Lieblich Piccolo	2
		Mixture (3 ranks)	
PEDAL		Cornopean	8
Acoustic Bass	32	Oboe	8
Bourdon	16	Tremulant	
Lieblich Bourdon	16		
Bass Flute	8		

COUPLERS: 3 unison; Swell octave
COMPASS: Manuals 56; Pedal 30
ACTION: electro-pneumatic

CHURCH OF ST PHILIP & ST JAMES, OVER HACKNEY

Enjoying a magnificent view over the valley, this so-called Mission Room was first built in 1913 and then totally rebuilt and modernised in the 1960's. It now represents a very pleasant little worship centre – homely, decently furnished and with excellent acoustics.

The small organ, uninspiring on paper, though surprisingly adequate on account of its location and acoustical surroundings, is by Abbott & Smith of Leeds and must date from the 1890's. Although it obviously must have come from somewhere else (– perhaps even a house), it gives the impression of being tailor-made for the building, both musically and visually.

GREAT		PEDAL	
Open Diapason	8	Bourdon	16
Dulciana	8*		
Viola	8*		
Lieblich Gedact	8*		
Gedact Flute	4*		

COUPLER: Manual to Pedal
COMPASS: Manual 56; Pedal 29
ACTION: mechanical
* stops enclosed in a swell

DALE ROAD METHODIST CHURCH (former Wesleyan)

The stylish Gothic front of this chapel next-door to the imposing Whitworth Institute is a familiar feature on the main A6 road through the Dale. Opened in 1904, it replaced an earlier Wesleyan chapel in the area east of the road, known as Two Dales.

What organ was here at first is not known. The present one came from a private residence and dates from the early years of the twentieth century. Built originally by P. Conacher of Huddersfield, it was installed in Dale Road Chapel by J.H. Adkins in 1943.

With its pneumatic action, its tablet stop-keys and its predominantly unison tone, it is clearly a totally Romantic instrument of quasi-orchestral type – an Edwardian style that is very much out of fashion nowadays. Nevertheless it has some beautiful tone qualities and deserves conservational care in order to preserve its undoubted musical character and effectiveness.

GREAT		SWELL	
Open Diapason	8	Viol d'Amour	8
Stopped Diapason	8	Rohr Flute	8
Gamba	8	Salicional	8
Harmonic Flute	4	Voix Celestes	8
		Principal	4
		Oboe	8
		Tremulant	

CHOIR		PEDAL	
Viol d'Orchestre	8	Bourdon	16
Dulciana	8	Bass Flute	8
Flute	4		
Flautina	2		
Clarinet	8 (enclosed in its own swell box)		

COUPLERS: unison, sub and octave
COMPASS: Manuals 56; Pedal 30
ACTION: pneumatic

HACKNEY METHODIST CHURCH (former Primitive)

The 1908 Gothic chapel replaces an earlier, very tiny one which can still be seen nearby.

The label on the organ reads: "Re-built & enlarged, J. Housley Adkins ... "
– an operation that could well have dated from the time of the opening of the new chapel. The organ's origins, however, are more likely to be around the 1870's or 80's. Some little pinnacled spheres on the corner posts of the case are slightly reminiscent of examples by J.M. Grunwell of Derby.

In 1990 a bottom octave of pipes was provided by J.H. Poyser for the previously Tenor-C compass Oboe.

GREAT		SWELL	
Open Diapason	8	Lieblich Gedact	8
Clarabella Flute	8	Gamba	8
Dulciana	8	Celeste	8
Flute	4	Salicet	4
		Oboe	8
PEDAL		Tremulant	
Bourdon	16		

COUPLERS: 3 unison
COMPASS: Manuals 56; Pedal 30
ACTION: Manuals mechanical; Pedal pneumatic

HILLSIDE METHODIST CHURCH (former Primitive)

Built in 1912, this chapel replaced an earlier one further up the valley, in Northwood. An old photograph of the interior shows a harmonium in use. Later a 2-manual pipe organ was installed by amateur enthusiasts but this was ultimately replaced by the present electronic instrument.

Derbyshire Organ Builders Represented In The Text

J.H. ADKINS
(also known as John H. Adkins and J. Housley Adkins)

Probably the most prolific of all Derbyshire's organ builders. He was indentured to J.M. Grunwell (qv) from 1884 to 1887. There then followed periods of working for White of Grantham and Denning of Stamford. In 1898 he returned to Derby and set up his own business in the disused former Wesleyan Chapel, St Michael's Lane. Before long he had taken over the practice of his master, Grunwell.

The best of his instruments (especially the earlier ones) had a sturdy Romantic quality, typical of the Edwardian period. Much of his work, though (inevitably), was in the nature of modifications and "improvements" to existing instruments, where his approach was not always sympathetic to the older material.

The firm lasted until 1958 when it was merged with J W Walker of London. They retained Mr J H Poyser (qv), grandson of J.H. Adkins, as their local Representative and Area Manager.

CHARLES EDEN

It has been said of him that "he only built one organ then went broke". Whatever the truth of this statement, the writer knows of at least four instruments on which he did some work, including two in the present survey. His address was given on the labels as "Derby" and he functioned from about 1900 until the Second World War.

JOSEPH GRATIAN

The earliest known resident organ builder in the county – apart from the two Strokes (qv) at Wirksworth in the sixteenth century. Born in 1784, he was a native of Belper, where his address is given in Pigot's 1835 Diectory as Chapel Street. Later Directories (in the 1840's and 50's) also give a Derby address: 56 Upper Brook Street. He died in 1863.

In Belper he did work at St John's and St Peter's as well as at the Congregational and Wesleyan Chapels, while in Derby he re-erected the Buckingham organ from old St Alkmund's in the newly-built Victorian church. He also appears to have worked as far away as Eastwood (Nottinghamshire).

Gratian was well thought of locally, not only for his organ activities but also apparently as a "silk-stockinger, grocer, tooth-drawer, poet and musician".

J.M. GRUNWELL

John Mitchell Grunwell had worked with William Hill in London before setting up on his own account in Traffic Street, Derby. Four of his instruments are represented in this survey – all dating from the 1870's. The business was eventually taken over in (or shortly after) 1898 by his one-time apprentice, J.H. Adkins (qv).

BERTRAM HOPKINSON

All we know of this builder from Ashover is that he "cleaned, repaired and tuned" the organ at Tansley in 1937 and added a Tremulant stop.

THE JOHNSON ORGAN COMPANY

Alan Johnson, formerly with J.H. Adkins, founded the Company in 1954. As was the case with Adkins, much of their work was necessarily in the rebuilding and modifying of existing instruments. They specialised in electric actions and built several new organs that used, either wholly or partially, the unit-extension principle. Following the death of Alan Johnson in 1992 the firm continued for a while under his son, Paul, but in 1994 merged with Henry Groves & Son of Nottingham.

ALFRED NOBLE

The father, Mark Noble, was established in Norwich following an apprenticeship with J.M. Holdich in London. His son, Alfred, worked in Norwich until 1870 when he moved to Derby (63 Melbourne Street), from where he pursued a trade nation-wide. This ceased in or about 1901, after which Alfred's son, William Thomas Noble, moved to London to continue in the business.

J H POYSER

John Housley Poyser was apprenticed to his grandfather, J.H. Adkins. When the family firm merged with J.W. Walker in 1958 he became Derbyshire Representative and then Area Manager of that firm. In 1975 he set up his own business in Derby, where he continues to undertake the overhauling, restoration or rebuilding of instruments of all types and sizes.

J SCOTCHBROOK

Jack Scotchbrook was officially employed by J.H. Adkins as well as by the Derby Carriage and Waggon Works. Unofficially, however, he indulged in minor extra-curricular organ maintenance activities on his own account. The only instrument actually bearing his name was at SS Augustine, Chesterfield, where the label read: "J. Scotchbrook & A.S. Johnson" and was dated "1952-1956" (– during which period, as we have seen above, Alan Johnson actually set up his own Company).

Scotchbrook's chief memorial is in the form of two notebooks in which he wrote down the specifications of all the instruments he visited – a useful source of information (idiosyncratic spelling apart!) for the period between the wars.

JOHN STACEY

Stacey had an address at 24 Bedford Street (–the terraced house still exists) and an entry is to be found in the Directories of 1895. He had formerly been with Brindley & Foster in Sheffield. His only remaining organ is at Tansley (1896).

E.R. STOW

Edmund Stow, formerly at the BR Technical Centre in Derby, had in his spare time (with volunteer assistance) worked on the restoration of a number of tracker instruments in Derby, Duffield and Belper. In 1994 he took voluntary severance from BR and now works professionally as an organ restorer.

STROKE

William and Nicholas Stroke are mentioned in the Calendar of Patent Rolls of 1503 as organ makers of "Wyrkesworth", Derbyshire.

THE SOURCES

For general architectural and historical information the following have proved to be invaluable:

Cooper, B., Transformation of a Valley. Heinemann, 1983. Reprinted Scarthin Books, 1991.

Drackley, The Revd. J. O., Notes on the Churches of Derbyshire. 1991.

Pevsner, N., The Buildings of England – Derbyshire (revised by E. Williamson). Penguin Books, reprinted with corrections and addenda, 1986.

Royal Commission on the Historical Monuments of England: An Inventory of Nonconformist Chapels and Meeting-Houses in Central England. HMSO, 1986.

In organ matters the most important historical document is undoubtedly the early nineteenth century notebook of Alexander Buckingham (itinerant organ builder) as published under the title of:

Buckingham's Travels. Edited by L. S. Barnard and serialized in "The Organ" quarterly review, Nos. 205-213, 1973-1975. There is reference to some twenty-six Derbyshire organs, of which eight are in the area covered by the present book.

Other nineteenth century sources include:

Austin, The Revd. M.R., The Church in Derbyshire in 1823-4. Derbyshire Archaeological Society Record Series, Vol. 5 for 1969-70. This reproduces the Parochial Visitation of Archdeacon Butler undertaken during those same years, making useful mention of twenty-seven organs in the County as a whole.

The Sperling Notebook – an important mid-nineteenth century document housed in the Library of the Royal College of Organists, London. Amongst other Derbyshire entries it contains references to instruments at Duffield and Belper.

Old Directories and micro-films of local newspapers in the Local Studies section of the Derbyshire Library Service.

The earlier part of the twentieth century is catered for with the following documents:

The accounts of J. H. Adkins for the years 1900-15 in the possession of Mr. J. H. Poyser of Derby. These contain nearly four hundred entries, though several (confusingly) are listed under the names of individuals representing the particular churches or chapels.

The Scotchbrook Notebooks. These two volumes of specifications are noted from the point of view of a tuner inside the instrument: their spellings and precise nomenclatures do not always reflect exactly what appears at the console. The first volume is in the possession of the Revd. J. Bland of Derby and deals with organs in Derby itself, apparently during the 1920's. The second one, going up to the end of the 1930's, covers the wider country area as well; it was formerly with the Johnson Organ Co. but is now lodged with Messrs H. Groves of Nottingham.

A further valuable source of information is the British Organ Archive, administered on behalf of the British Institute of Organ Studies by its Archivist, Mr. D.C. Wickens.

Other published material containing references to organs in the area:

Barrass, G., Methodism in Belper. Fleet Press, Belper, 1993.

Barton, D.A., Around Matlock in old Photographs. Alan Sutton Publishing, in collaboration with Derbyshire County Council, 1993.

Boston, The Revd. Canon N.: see Langwill and Boston.

Downes, R., Baroque Tricks. Positif Press, 1983. As well as reminiscing about organs in Derby itself he has some interestingly appreciative comments about the organ builder, J.H. Adkins.

Drackley, The Revd. J.O., Matlock Parish Church. The Church Publishers, Ramsgate, 1981.

Drackley, The Revd. J.O., All Saints' Church Turnditch. Privately published, no date.

Elvin, L., Forster and Andrews : Their Barrel, Chamber and Small Church Organs. Laurence Elvin, Lincoln, 1976.

Fletcher, G.A., Records of Wesleyan Methodism in the Belper Circuit, 1760-1903. Belper, 1903.

Fletcher, G.A., 150 Years of Music in the Wesleyan Methodist Church, Belper, 1780-1930. Condensed version of original manuscript printed in Methodist "The Choir", August 1931.

Friend, The Revd. F.A., Historical Notes on St. Peter's, Belper. Manuscript, C19th.

Gaskell, D., Holy Trinity Church Tansley. Privately published, 1990.

Gilfillan, F.A., The Things They Said. "The Organ" quarterly review, No. 262, October 1987. An article about "Scudamore" Chancel Organs.

Langwill, L. G. and Boston, The Revd. Canon N., Church and Chamber Barrel-Organs. Lyndesay G. Langwill, Edinburgh, revised and enlarged, 1970.

Makin, D., Music in Belper (1824-1975). Privately published, 1975.

Matthews, B., Travellers' Tales (from the Diaries of John Byng and others). British Institute of Organ Studies (BIOS) Journal No. 17, 1993.

National Pipe Organ Register. Trial print-out, BIOS, 1993.

Oldknow, H., United Methodist Church, Milford, Jubilee 1859-1909. Published privately, 1909.

Peters, D., Darley Abbey from monastery to industrial community. Moorland, 1974.

Sayer, M., Samuel Renn English Organ Builder. Phillimore, 1974.

Smith, The Revd. D., Belper Unitarian Chapel. Published privately, revised, 1994.

Stow, E.R., The History and Restoration of the Organ in St. Peter's Church Belper. Published privately, 1979; also printed in "The Organ" quarterly review, No. 233, July 1980.

Sumner, W. L., The Organ. Macdonald and Jane's, fourth edition, 1973.

Tomkins, R., The Pipe Organ at Openwoodgate Church, Belper. "The Organ" quarterly review, No. 265, July 1988.

Watson, W. R., The Illustrated History of Duffield. Chevin Books, Duffield, 1986.

Willott, C., Belper and its People. Belper, 1894.

INDEX OF ORGAN BUILDERS

J.H. ADKINS (Derby)

ALLESTREE	St. Edmund
BELPER	Christ Church
	Congregational
	Methodist Central
	Methodist Pottery
	Methodist Salem
	Public Hall
	St. Mark, Openwoodgate
	St. Peter
BREADSALL	All Saints
CRICH	Baptist
	St. Mary
CROMFORD	Methodist
DARLEY DALE	Methodist Dale Road
	Methodist Hackney
	St. Helen
DUFFIELD	Methodist Chapel Street
	Methodist King Street
HEAGE	Methodist Ebenezer
HOLBROOK	Methodist
	St. Michael
KIRK IRETON	Holy Trinity
LITTLE EATON	Methodist
MATLOCK	Congregational Farley Hill
	Methodist Bank Road (Primitive)
	Methodist Imperial Road
	Methodist Starkholmes
	Methodist/URC Bank Road
	URC Chesterfield Road
MIDDLETON	Congregational
	Methodist Main Street
MILFORD	Baptist
	Methodist Chevin Road
	Methodist Shaw Lane
OPENWOODGATE	(see Belper)
QUARNDON	St. Paul
SOUTH DARLEY	St. Mary
TURNDITCH	All Saints
WENSLEY	(see South Darley)
WIRKSWORTH	Baptist
	Methodist

ABBOTT & SMITH (Leeds)

DARLEY DALE	St. Philip & St. James Over Hackney

WILLIAM ANDREWS (Bradford)

HOLLOWAY	Christ Church

GEORGE BENSON (Manchester)

BELPER	Jubilee Hall
MATLOCK	Congregational Farley Hill

BEVERLEY & WILLIAMS (Stockport)
MIDDLETON   Methodist Mount Zion

BEVINGTON & SONS (London)
BELPER   Convent
IDRIDGEHAY   St. James
LITTLE EATON   Methodist
MATLOCK   Methodist/URC
MATLOCK BATH Holy Trinity
MILFORD   Holy Trinity

J.J. BINNS (Leeds)
BELPER   St. Peter

J.C. BISHOP (London)
HOLBROOK   Methodist

BRINDLEY & FOSTER (Sheffield)
ALDERWASLEY   All Saints
BELPER   Christ Church
        Public Hall
DARLEY DALE   St. Helen
MATLOCK   Methodist Bank Road (Primitive)
        St. Giles
WIRKSWORTH   St. Mary

ALEXANDER BUCKINGHAM (London)
ALDERWASLEY   St. Margaret
BELPER   St. Mark, Openwoodgate
BREADSALL   All Saints
CROMFORD   St. Mary
DARLEY ABBEY   St. Matthew
DUFFIELD   St. Alkmund
OPENWOODGATE (see Belper)
WIRKSWORTH   St. Mary

HAROLD CANTRILL (Castle Donongton)
ALLESTREE   St. Nicholas
QUARNDON   St. Paul

THOMAS CASSON (see The Positive Organ Co. Ltd.)

PETER CONACHER & Co. (Huddersfield)
DARLEY DALE   Methodist Dale Road

JOHN CORKHILL (Wigan)
DARLEY ABBEY   St. Matthew

COUSANS, SONS & Co./COUSANS (LINCOLN) Ltd.
BELPER   Methodist Central
DUFFIELD   St. Alkmund
WIRKSWORTH   RC Our Lady & St. Teresa

JOHN DAVIS (Cleobury Mortimer)
CRICH   Methodist Crich Carr

CHARLES EDEN (Derby)
 MILFORD   Methodist Ebenezer
 QUARNDON   St. Paul

ELLIOT & HILL (London)
 WIRKSWORTH   St. Mary

GEORGE ENGLAND (or GEORGE PIKE ENGLAND) (London)
 DARLEY ABBEY   St. Matthew

FAULKNER BROS (Manchester)
 BELPER   Methodist Central

T. W. FEARN (London)
 WIRKSWORTH   URC

FLIGHT (& ROBSON) (London)
 BREADSALL   All Saints
 MATLOCK   St. Giles
 TANSLEY   Holy Trinity

FORSTER & ANDREWS (Hull)
 DARLEY ABBEY   St. Matthew
 DUFFIELD   Methodist King Street
 MATLOCK   All Saints
 TANSLEY   Holy Trinity
 WIRKSWORTH   St. Mary

JOSEPH GRATIAN (Belper and Derby)
 BELPER   Congregational
                         Methodist Central
                         St. John
                         St. Peter
 DUFFIELD   Methodist Chapel Street

GRAY & DAVISON (London)
 DUFFIELD   St. Alkmund

HENRY GROVES & SON (Nottingham)
 ALLESTREE   St. Edmund
 BONSALL   St. James
 DARLEY DALE   St. Helen
 MATLOCK   Methodist/URC

J.M. GRUNWELL (Derby)
 BELPER   Baptist
                         St. Peter
 CRICH   Baptist
 DARLEY DALE   Methodist Hackney
 HEAGE   Methodist Nether Heage
 MATLOCK   Methodist Starkholmes
 MILFORD   Holy Trinity
 QUARNDON   St. Paul
 WIRKSWORTH   URC

JAMES HANCOCK (London)
    DUFFIELD   St. Alkmund

HARDY & SON (Stockport)
    BELPER   Methodist Field Head
                               Methodist Zion, Openwoodgate
    OPENWOODGATE (see Belper)

W. HEDGELAND (London)
    HEAGE   St. Luke

ANTHONY HERROD (Skegby)
    HEAGE   St. Luke

W. HILL & SON (London) (see also Elliot & Hill)
    ALLESTREE   St. Edmund
    CRICH   St. Mary
    CROMFORD   St. Mary
    HOLBROOK   St. Michael
    MATLOCK BATH   Holy Trinity

WILLIAM HOLT (Bradford)
    BELPER   St. Peter

BERTRAM HOPKINSON (Ashover)
    TANSLEY   Holy Trinity

JARDINE & Co./JARDINE CHURCH ORGANS (Manchester)
    AMBERGATE   Methodist
    BONSALL   St. James
    TURNDITCH   All Saints

The JOHNSON ORGAN COMPANY (Derby)
    DUFFIELD   Baptist
                               Methodist King Street
    HAZELWOOD   St John
    KIRK IRETON   Holy Trinity
    MATLOCK   Congregational Farley Hill
    MILFORD   Methodist Shaw Lane
    TANSLEY   Holy Trinity

ALBERT KEATES (Sheffield)
    CROMFORD   Lady Glenorchy's Chapel

KINGSGATE DAVIDSON & Co. Ltd. (London)
    WIRKSWORTH   St. Mary

ALFRED KIRKLAND (London)
    KIRK IRETON   Holy Trinity
    LITTLE EATON   St. Paul

C. LLOYD & Co. (Nottingham)

BELPER	Congregational
	Convent
BONSALL	St. James
CROMFORD	St. Mary
HAZELWOOD	St. John
HOLLOWAY	Methodist
MATLOCK	Methodist Imperial Road
	URC Chesterfield Road
MATLOCK BATH	Methodist
MIDDLETON	Congregational
	Holy Trinity

MIDLAND ORGAN BUILDERS (Beeston)

MATLOCK	All Saints

NELSON & Co. (Durham)

BELPER	Methodist Central
	St. Swithun

NICHOLSON & LORD (Walsall)

DUFFIELD	Baptist
	St. Alkmund

ALFRED NOBLE (Derby)

ALLESTREE	St. Edmund
MIDDLETON	Methodist Main Street
MILFORD	Methodist Ebenezer
TURNDITCH	All Saints

The POSITIVE ORGAN Co. (London)

BELPER	St. Laurence Convent
DETHICK	St. John

J. H. POYSER (Derby)

ALDERWASLEY	All Saints
DARLEY DALE	Methodist Hackney
HOLBROOK	St. Michael
LITTLE EATON	Methodist
QUARNDON	St. Paul
SOUTH DARLEY	St. Mary
WENSLEY	(see South Darley)

RADCLIFFE & SAGAR (Leeds)

BELPER	St. Peter

MARTIN RENSHAW (Lyminge)

BELPER	St. Mark, Openwoodgate

W.E. RICHARDSON & SONS (Manchester)

HEAGE	Methodist Parkside

JOHANN SNETZLER (London)
BELPER	St. John
	St. Peter
HEAGE	St. Luke

JOHN STACEY (Derby)
TANSLEY	Holy Trinity

STEELE & KEAY (Burslem)
ALLESTREE	St. Nicholas

E.R. STOW (Derby)
BELPER	Methodist Zion, Openwoodgate
	St. Peter
DUFFIELD	Methodist King Street
MATLOCK	Methodist Starkholmes
MILFORD	Holy Trinity
OPENWOODGATE	(see Belper)

WILLIAM & NICHOLAS STROKE (Wirksworth)
WIRKSWORTH	St. Mary

M.C. THOMPSON (Burton-on-Trent)
ALLESTREE	St. Nicholas
AMBERGATE	Methodist
BELPER	Christ Church
HOLLOWAY	Christ Church

WADSWORTH & BRO. (Manchester)
BREADSALL	All Saints
SOUTH DARLEY	St. Mary
WENSLEY	(see South Darley)

J.W. WALKER & SONS (London)
MATLOCK	All Saints

STEPHEN (or STEVEN) WHITE (London)
BELPER	St. Mark, Openwoodgate
BREADSALL	All Saints
OPENWOODGATE	(see Belper)

HENRY WILLIS (London)
BREADSALL	All Saints
CROMFORD	St. Mary
KIRK IRETON	Holy Trinity

WOOD OF HUDDERSFIELD
ALLESTREE	St. Edmund
BELPER	St. Peter
DUFFIELD	St. Alkmund

ALEXANDER YOUNG & SONS (Manchester)
AMBERGATE	St. Anne

INDEX OF PERSONS
(OTHER THAN ORGAN BUILDERS)

Index Of Places

The publishers thank the following and other, unlisted subscribers for their confidence in, and support of, this book.

Andrew Abbott
Jenny Acons
The Rt. Revd. Jonathan S. Bailey
Marion E. Ball
Stuart Bassett
Mr. T. W. Beamond (2)
Lady Bemrose
Terence W. Bennett
Jim Berrow
John W. Birkby
The Revd. John D. Bland
Anthony J. Boden
J.J. Boughton
Ralph Bootman
Mr. O.W. Brittain
Nigel Browne
John W. Bullimore
Peter Bumstead
D.R. Carrington
M.A. Chamberlain
Barrie Clark
The Council for the Care of Churches
Macdonald Coventry
Canon C.H. Davidson
E. Glyn Davies
The Bishop of Derby (2)
Derby Cathedral
Derbyshire Library Service (6)
The Revd. J.O. Drackley
David Drinkell
Bernard B. Edmonds
Ken Ellis
Laurence Elvin, FSA (2)
Aidan Evans
Dr. Paul Faunch
Simon Fitzgerald
D.R.S. Force
Denys Gaskell
David Gedge
Dr. Richard Godfrey
The Revd. J.F.B. Goodwin
P.A. Graham
Paul Hale, Organist's Review
Mr. Robin Halls

Hallwood Library, University of Nottingham
A. Herrod
Roy W. Honeywell
Geoffrey Howell
Ken Hunt
Alastair Johnston
B.R. Jones
Mr. K. Jones
Len Krause
Denis Littleton
Anthony Lodge

St Mary's Church, Nottingham
Wirksworth
Bishop Designate of Derby
Tansley
Breaston
Whatstandwell
Hazelwood
Oakwood
Edgbaston
Duffield
Littleover
Market Drayton
Wallingford
Stoke Holy Cross
Wokingham
Haverfordwest
Thornhill, Dewsbury
Organ Builder, Ipswich
Lytham St. Annes
Burrough on the Hill
Reigate

Wootton Bassett
Roade
Calver

Matlock
Belfast Cathedral
Needham Market
Dronfield Parish Church
Swanpool, Lincoln
Newcastle-Upon-Tyne
London WC2
Stamford Brook, London
Herstmonceux
Tansley
Brecon
Salisbury DAC
Belper
Meopham
Southwell
Organist and Director of Music, St. Mary Magdalen's Church, Brighton

Organ Builder, Skegby
Northampton
Darley Abbey
Sandiacre
Frome, Somerset
Huddersfield
Derby
Pinner
Ripley
Mareham Le Fen

William Madin	*Tideswell*
John R. Maidment	*Wokingham*
Frederick T. Mansfield, MBE	*Derby*
K.H. Mantell	*Duffield*
Dr. Roy Massey	*Cathedral Close, Hereford*
Matlock Methodist & United Reformed Church	
Alden R. Morcom	*Camberley*
William Morgan, BA, FRCO	*Firwood, Bolton*
John Norman	*London N20*
Colin Osman	*Cockfosters*
Barbara Owen	*Newburyport, MA, USA*
Mrs. M. Daphne Parsons	*Farnah Green*
A.G. Peel	*Beeston, Nottinghamshire*
David Pether	*Wokingham*
Paul Pickerill	*West Heath, Birmingham*
N.M. Plumley, Esq, MA, FRSA	*Arundel*
K.F. Plummer	*Belper*
Steve Porter (2)	*Organist, Matlock St Giles*
J.H. Poyser, MISOB	*Organ Builder, Derby*
D.M. Pratt	*Shelton Lock*
Mr. and Mrs. R. Price	*Weston-on-Trent*
R.C.D. Rees	*Leicester*
Martin Renshaw	*Abbaretz, France*
Doreen Rickards	*Bonsall*
Mr. D.J. Roome	*Belper*
Mr. Gerald Roper, ARCM	*Organist of St. Osmund's Church, Parkstone*
M.A. Sale	*Exeter*
John Sears	*West Bridgford*
B.C. Shepherd & Son (2)	*Edgware*
David Shepherd	*Holbeach*
L.W. Slade	*Duffield*
William Smallman	*Condover*
Mr. G.R. Smith	*Stapleford*
Mr. E.A. Spencer	*South Wingfield*
Mrs. B.M. Sykes	*Pilsley*
Mrs. Marion Taulbut	*Duffield*
The Revd. Nicholas Thistlethwaite	*Trumpington*
A.F. Thoday	*Holloway*
M.C. Thompson	*Organ Builder, Stretton, Burton on Trent*
Paul Tindall	*Gants Hill*
Mrs. A.L. Tomkins	*Duffield*
Leslie Townsend	*Canterbury*
Professor Peter Tregenza	*Grindleford*
Faith Troche	*Duffield*
R.P. and E.A. Turville (2)	*Nether Heage*
John Wallis	*Heage*
N.G. Walmsley	*Harrogate*
Mr. M.R. Warson	*Northampton*
Raymond Watmore	*Hailsham*
Dr. D.T. Wells	*Allestree*
Bob Wetton	*Bournemouth*
T.M.N. Whitehall	*Wisbech*
Jack L. Whiteley	*Lymm*
Dr. John K. Whittle	*St. Mary's Church, Nottingham*
Richard Wood	*Allestree*
D.J. Woodward	*Duffield*
J. Wilbur Wright (2)	*Oxford*

SCARTHIN BOOKS
HISTORY TITLES IN PRINT 1995

St John's Chapel, Belper
The Life of a Church and a Community
E.G. Power
The history of "The Foresters' Chapel" and the people it served, from the 13th century to the present. This book is not a guidebook for the antiquarian, but easy reading for anyone interested in the past life of Belper and the place of St John's Chapel in that life. 40pp. ISBN 0 907758 11 8

Our Village
Alison Uttley's Cromford
Alison Uttley
Cromford, well-known as the site of the world's first water-powered cotton mill, is also fortunate to have as its chronicler the celebrated essayist and children's writer, Alison Uttley. This collection of essays vividly recalls scenes from the self-sufficient late Victorian village of her childhood. Illustrated by C.F. Tunnicliffe. 72pp. ISBN 0 907758 08 8

The Crich Tales
Unexpurgated Echoes from a Derbyshire Village
Geoffrey Dawes
Tales of earthy humour and rural shrewdness, told in a village pub. Illustrations by Geoff Taylor. 96pp. ISBN 0 907758 06 1

Hanged for a Sheep
Crime in Bygone Derbyshire
E.G. Power
A factual and entertaining survey of crime and the fight against it from 1750 to 1850. 80pp. ISBN 0 907758 00 2

Walls Across the Valley
The Building of the Howden and Derwent Dams
Brian Robinson
An illustrated history of the work of the Derwent Valley Water Board, produced in collaboration with Severn Trent Water. Contains a wealth of previously unpublished photographs and diagrams, also 20 colour photographs. Of particular interest to students of social, railway and engineering history. 256pp Appendices, bibliography, index, duotone and colour illustrations. ISBN 0 907758 57 6

Waterways to Derby
A study of the Derwent Navigation and Derby Canal
Celia M. Swainson
The battle to link Derby to the arteries of trade during the Industrial Revolution. 64pp. ISBN 0 907758 59 2

Historic Farmhouses around Derby
Barbara Hutton
A detailed study of the old brick and timber farmhouses of South Derbyshire and the Trent Valley. Full gazetteer/index. 64pp. ISBN 0 907758 48 7

Millclose: the Mine that Drowned
Lynn Willies, Keith Gregory, Harry Parker
The story of Britain's largest-ever lead mine and the men who worked it. 59 illustrations. 64pp. ISBN 0 907758 28 2

The Seven Blunders of the Peak
A fresh look at some Derbyshire legends
edited by Brian Robinson
. . . or Derbyshire de-bunked. Derbyshire is rich in history and legend, not all based on fact. Seven well-known Derbyshire writers and historians put the record straight. ISBN 0 907758 77 0

The Cromford Guide
Freda Bayles and Janet Ede
Based on three walks around the village and the surrounding countryside, *The Cromford Guide* points out the many features of interest past and present in this lively village. 48pp 5 maps + photographs. ISBN 0 907758 76 2

Transformation of a Valley
Brian Cooper & Neville Cooper
The lively and scholarly story of the Derwent Valley during the development of mines, mills and other industries. The most readable and authoritative guide to the industrial history of the area. With maps and 130 photographs of historic sites. Bibliography, index. 316pp. ISBN 0 907758 17 7

Derbyshire in the Civil War
Brian Stone
The only single-volume work on the subject. It traces the fighting in Derbyshire and the deeds of Derbyshire men elsewhere, and also looks at the plight of non-combatants and the personal animosities motivating leaders on both sides. Illustrated, with notes, bibliography and index. 157pp. ISBN 0 907758 58 4

Robert Bakewell: Artist Blacksmith
S. Dunkerley
Thirty-two pages of colour photographs with opposing pages of commentary form the core of this unique life of the great 18th century craftsman in wrought iron. Bound in high-quality cloth. With line drawings, gazetteer and index. Limited to 750 signed copies. 112pp. ISBN 0 907758 24 X

The Clay Cross Calamities
Terry Judge
Miners' lives and the struggle for coal in Victorian Derbyshire, written by a deep miner and local historian.
112pp. ISBN 0 907758 79 7

Scarthin Books are particularly interested in publishing scholarly work with a strong local and specialised national appeal. We are also leading second-hand and antiquarian booksellers with a strong interest in music and a constant need to purchase good scores and books. Our whimsical leaflet is available free of charge. Contacts: Dr. D.J. Mitchell, Dr. G.N. Cooper.